BEEF
SWITZERLAND

THE MOST REFRESHING WAY TO DISCOVER SWITZERLAND

Beer Hiking Switzerland
The Most Refreshing Way to Visit Switzerland
By Monika Saxer

ISBN: 978-2-940481-13-2

Published by Helvetiq
Illustrations by: Lisa Voisard - Agathe Altwegg
Roxanne Borloz - Cécile Gretsch - Lucas Guidetti
Copy-editing by: Marie-Claude Hirnisberger - Nathalie Ré
Printed in 2015
First Edition October 2015
Second Edition November 2019

www.helvetiq.com
www.facebook.com/helvetiq

BEER HIKING
SWITZERLAND

THE MOST REFRESHING WAY TO DISCOVER SWITZERLAND

HELVETIQ

A big thank you to Philippe Corbat, who evaluated many beers for us and allowed us to benefit from his extensive knowledge of the "landscape" of Swiss beer.

TABLE OF CONTENTS

INTRODUCTION

ABOUT MONIKA

Monika Saxer has been a hiking enthusiast since her earliest days. As a hiking guide at SAC Baldern, she is often looking for new mountain hikes. Although she always sets off with one and a half liters of tea in her backpack, she is still thirsty enough after a hike for a cold beer. As more and more craft breweries have opened, places serving local beer have become her favorite destinations. This book is a compilation of her original hiking ideas for beer enthusiasts. Of course, these hikes are also available to those of you who don't drink!

ABOUT THE BOOK

When I learned to walk, a world full of adventures and marvels was waiting for me outside. I would walk with other children across the fields and forests around the village. Fortunately, I wasn't held back by my parents, unlike most young girls. On the contrary, we never had boring family walks, we had mountain hikes and camping vacations, as well as overnight stays in mountain huts.

When I left home, I became a member of Club Alpin des femmes de Zurich (Women's Alpine Club of Zurich), now called CAS section Baldern. I quickly learned to appreciate a good beer after a hike. At that time, drinking beer was even more enjoyable because it wasn't a "women's" activity.

Soon afterwards I was asked at the club, "Why don't you also become a hiking guide?" So, I learned how to read a map and I began guiding exploration hikes.

A newspaper article about the opening of the first traditional microbrewery in Switzerland inspired me to finish a hike in Basel, at the Fischerstube. From time to time I heard about the opening of a new brewery and I imagined a new hike to get there.

Suddenly, everything went quickly. Breweries were opening everywhere. I had just taken responsibility for the association's website and was truly enjoying developing it.

This is what gave me the idea to put my beer hikes online. A journalist from the club Illauer Punt took part in the project.

When I described a hike from Tösstal to Illnau to discover their local beer, she asked me to have an interview with *Migros Magazine* about women and beer.

This article on my beer hikes caught the attention of the publishing house Helvetiq and we decided to write a book about them. You can find any Swiss brewery by searching the list of taxable national breweries kept by the Federal Finance Department. I check the internet to see which beer will be available and when. After checking the weather forecast, I choose the area in which I want to hike. Then, all I have to do is study the maps, the itinerary and set my alarm clock. My life partner, who also enjoys a good beer, is with me most of the time. While writing this book, I also had the opportunity to take a glimpse at the world of publishing.

HERE'S HOW IT WORKS!

CHOOSE THE BEER OR THE HIKE ①

NAME OF THE HIKE
CANTON
NAME OF THE BEER
MAP*

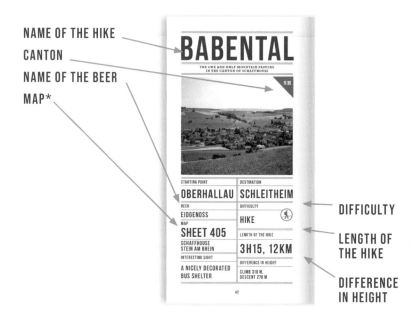

DIFFICULTY

LENGTH OF THE HIKE

DIFFERENCE IN HEIGHT

* The 'sheets' refer to the official maps of «Swiss hiking» which you can buy on the Internet:

www.toposhop.admin.ch/fr/shop/products/maps/ leisure/hike/hiking

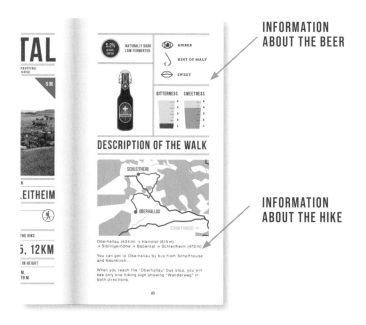

INFORMATION ABOUT THE BEER

INFORMATION ABOUT THE HIKE

THE DIFFICULTIES

The classification is determined by the most difficult parts of the hike. The sections which are particularly difficult are mentioned in the description of the itinerary. The difficulty is determined based on good weather conditions.
Poor weather, snow or ice can increase the difficulty.

WALKS
The footpaths are wide and the slope has a slight incline. If they are not muddy due to long periods of rain, you can even push an all-terrain stroller. The steps are indicated. The signs and markings are yellow.

HIKES
The hiking trails are paths that are clearly visible with little risk of falling. You can wear light-weight walking shoes. Dangerous sections are secured by a railing. Walkways or bridges cross the streams. The signs and markings are yellow.

ALPINE HIKES
Mountain trails are mostly steep and narrow. They can be hidden in some places and can lead to difficult terrain. Certain areas can present a risk of falling.
You many need to use your hands in order to keep your balance. Your feet may get wet crossing streams. These hikes require sturdy shoes with skid-proof soles. It's necessary to be surefooted, not to be afraid of heights, and to know the dangers of the mountains (weather, risks of slipping, falling rocks). The signposts and markings are white – red – white.

(2) BEFORE SETTING OFF

CHECK YOUR EQUIPMENT

 WEATHER

Detailed weather forecasts are available at:

→ www.meteoswiss.admin.ch.

→ By telephone: 162 (CHF 0.50 per call + CHF 0.50 per minute + additional fees).

→ On the radio: station SRF 1 at about 12:20 pm (in dialect).

→ On television: channel SRF 1 after the news at 7:30 pm (in dialect).

→ On television: channel RTS 1 after the news at 7:30 pm.

→ Individual information: everyday, 24 hours a day at 0900 162 333. Cost from a landline: CHF 3.00 per call + CHF 1.50 per minute.

HOW TO GET TO THE STARTING POINT

All the hikes are easily reached by public transportation.
The times and itineraries can be verified at www.sbb.ch.

PATH CONDITIONS AND SNOW

The network of hiking trails is created and maintained by associations of volunteers. There is no official service providing information about the current conditions of the trails.

It is preferable to contact the local tourism office if you have any questions.

A list of addresses can be found at www.wandersite.ch in the section "Verschiedenes" (in German or English).

The Study Institute of Snow and Avalanches provides information on snow conditions at www.slf.ch/en.

3

THE BEER HIKES

AIRPORT

BETWEEN PLANES AND THE RIED

ZH

STARTING POINT	**DESTINATION**
# NIEDERGLATT	ZURICH AIRPORT
BEER	**DIFFICULTY**
ZURICH AIRPORT BEER	
MAP	WALK
# SHEET 215	**LENGTH OF THE WALK**
(BADEN)	# 2H45, 11KM
INTERESTING SIGHT	**DIFFERENCE IN HEIGHT**
## LA PORTE DORÉE	CLIMB 60 M, DESCENT 50 M
RISING UNDERGROUND WATER	

5.8% ALCOHOL CONTENT

NON-FILTERED
NATURALLY
CLOUDY
TOP-FERMENTED

DARK GOLD

FRUITY

MALTY

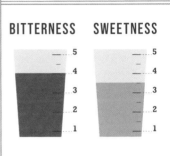

BITTERNESS   SWEETNESS

DESCRIPTION OF THE JOURNEY

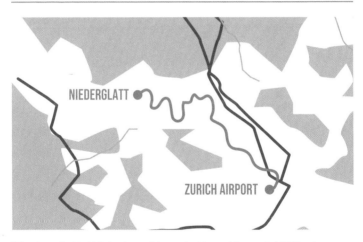

NIEDERGLATT

ZURICH AIRPORT

Niederglatt (424 m) → Oberglatt → Airport (430 m)

You can get to Niederglatt with the Zurich S-Bahn.

From the station in Niederglatt, go towards the Glatt River. When you arrive at the river, turn right in the direction of Oberglatt. Follow the twists and turns of the river upstream until the wood-covered bridge in Oberglatt. Turn left here, in the direction of Kloten.

After crossing a few streets in the area, you reach the

main road which links Oberglatt to Bachenbülasch.
Cross the road and continue straight on to the dirt
path. After about 400 meters, you arrive at an
intersection without a signpost. There, take the dirt
path to the right, this will lead you to the main road.
Cross the road again. There is a parking lot with
benches and a bistro at the end of the airport runway.
People fond of airplanes meet here, with camcorders,
binoculars, and radios in order to watch
the landing planes.

For the uninitiated, there are information signs about
the different types of airplanes. The trail follows the
fence around the airport then leads to the tank runway
on the Bülach-Kloten military premises. After about
400 meters, leave the tank path and turn right. If the
army is carrying out exercises, the runway is closed.
The rest of the time, it's a cyclists' paradise. More
information is available by calling 0448159645. Once
you've left the tank path, cross the wet biotope of
Halbmatt until you arrive back at the airport fence.
The trail once again runs alongside the fence. To the
right, you can watch the landing planes, and to the
left you can see the wonderful landscape of the
marsh. After about half an hour, you can make a
detour to the left to go to Porte Dorée. It's a pond
formed by rising underground water. Since the bottom
of the pond is made up of sand, you can see bubbling
water as it rises. Lots of frogs have made it their
home.

It only takes 10 minutes to go there and come back.
Once back on the trail in the direction of Kloten, it
takes 10 minutes to get to la Rega. Here, you leave
the trail and continue following the road, always in the
same direction. Continue alongside the airport for
another ten minutes until you reach a multi-lane street
with lights. From here, head towards Glattalbahn
(white trail sign) until the bus stop Fracht. Continue
on the same sidewalk past a tunnel-shaped metal
building until you reach the bus stop OPC. Turn right.
You'll see the Radisson Blu hotel on the other side of
the street. Cross by the motorcycle parking area and
head to the hotel entrance. The bar in the reception
area serves Zurich Airport Bier. If your order is met
with a blank look, try asking for it by its popular
acronym ZAB.

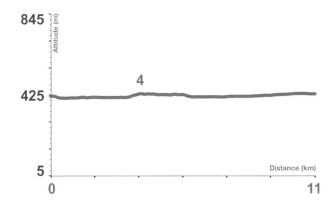

RETURN

Directly from the hotel bar and via an underground passage, you can get to the train station at the airport and a bus stop for post buses, regional buses and trains for the Glatt Valley.

SNACKBAR AM PISTENENDE OBERGLATT
078 757 31 98

RESTAURANT STOPOVER
Operation Center 4
8058 Zurich Flughafen
079 691 85 04
stopover@sv-group.ch

RADISSON BLU
Zürich Flughafen
8058 Zürich
044 800 40 40
www.radissonhotels.com/en-us/hotels/radisson-blu-zurich-airport

ZURICH AIRPORT BEER
www.flughafenbier.ch

INTERESTING SIGHTS
- La Porte Dorée, rising underground water
- Observation deck at the airport

AIGUILLES DE BAULMES

A RIDGE IN THE JURA RANGE WITH A LITTLE CLIMBING TO VISIT A CAVE

VD

STARTING POINT	**DESTINATION**
## STE-CROIX	## STE-CROIX
BEER	**DIFFICULTY**
LA FRAÎCHEUR	
MAP	ALPINE HIKE
SHEET 241	
(VAL DE TRAVERS)	**LENGTH OF THE ALPINE HIKE**
	5H, 16KM
INTERESTING SIGHT	**DIFFERENCE IN HEIGHT**
CREUX DES NEIGES GIANT SINKHOLE	CLIMB 680 M, DESCENT 680 M

5.0% ALCOHOL CONTENT

NON-FILTERED

 BLONDE, SLIGHTLY WHITE

 BITTER ORANGE PEEL

 REFRESHING

BITTERNESS   **SWEETNESS**

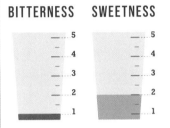

DESCRIPTION OF THE JOURNEY

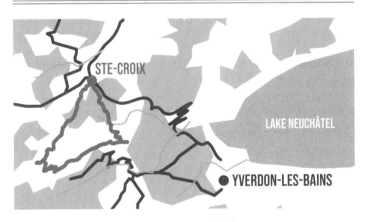

Ste-Crolx (1066 m) → Mont des Certs
→ La Gitte Dessous → La Gitte Dessus
→ Creux des Neiges Col de l'Aiguillon
→ Aiguilles de Baulmes (1559 m) → Cave Noire
→ Mont de Baulmes → Ste-Croix

You can get to Sainte-Croix by train from Yverdon or by post bus from Buttes (Val de Travers). This tour can be combined with the hike that crosses the Gorges of Covatanne (spending a night at Hôtel de France).

From the station in Sainte-Croix, follow the hiking trail leading up through the village towards the Col des Etroits. Shortly after the post bus stop at Avenue de Neuchâtel, turn left and go by the Mont des Cerfs, with its vast Jura meadows, until the mountain restaurant of La Gittaz Dessous.

To go from La Gittaz Dessous to La Gittaz Dessus, take a small road in the direction of Col de l'Aiguillon. At La Gittaz Dessus, leave the small road and turn right. From here, you will follow an unpaved shortcut until Col de l'Aiguillon. On this path you can make a small detour for the Creux des Neiges. It's an impressive sinkhole in the forest.

A winding path takes you from the Col de l'Aiguillon to the summit of the Aiguilles de Baulmes. You suddenly find yourself at a panoramic viewpoint above an almost vertical rock face. Below, you can see the lakes at the foot of the Jura Mountains and on the horizon, the Alpine range until Mont Blanc. From the summit, follow the ridge in the direction of Mont de Baulmes, going from viewpoint to viewpoint.
At pt. 1432 you can reach the entrance to the Cave Noire by crossing a rocky narrow gap and then walking along a ledge. It's imperative that you use the handrail for this passage. If you have a flashlight, you can explore the cave which is about 20 meters long. You will have to climb over some boulders and crawl around a few bends. Sometimes you have to lower your head or crouch down.
You suddenly come into the main room of the cave. Daylight shines into it through a light shaft. Turn around and go back to leave the cave and return to the ridge.
A small path to the left of the trail leads you quickly to a hole with a view of the cave from above. The hole is partially hidden in the forest floor.

After the cave adventure, follow the path of the ridge until Mont de Baulmes where there is a panoramic viewpoint and a mountain bistro. From there, go down through the forest to a small marsh and follow the train tracks to return to Sainte-Croix.

The beers at the brewery Trois Dames are available in several restaurants in Sainte-Croix. This hike goes to the Hôtel de France because they serve four different types of beer and you can spend the night. To get there, go up the street La Sagne until the avenue Les Alpes and then bear right until the Hôtel de France, which is about five minutes from the station.

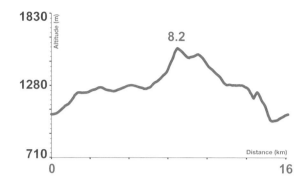

RETURN

The descent by train to Yverdon is an exceptional experience and very special. But the bus ride from Col des Etroits to Buttes followed by the train at the Val de Travers is also magnificent.

CAFÉ DE LA GITTAZ
La Gittaz-dessous
024 454 38 38
www.lagittaz.com

RESTAURANT DU MONT-DE-BAULMES
024 454 24 89

HÔTEL DE FRANCE
rue Centrale 25
1450 Ste-Croix/VD
024 454 38 21
www.hotelfrance.ch

BIÈRE TROIS DAMES
rue de France 1
1450 Ste-Croix/VD
024 454 43 75
www.brasserietroisdames.ch

INTERESTING SIGHTS
- Le Creux des Neiges, an impressive sinkhole
- La Cave Noire, a cave that can be reached with little effort.

AJOIE

DISCOVER SWITZERLAND'S YOUNGEST CANTON

JU

STARTING POINT	DESTINATION
ST-URSANNE	**PORRENTRUY**

BEER	DIFFICULTY
L'EAU DE ROSE	**WALK**

MAP	
SHEET 222	LENGTH OF THE WALK
(CLOS DU DOUBS)	**5H30, 21KM**

INTERESTING SIGHT	
THE OLD TOWNS ST-URSANNE AND PORRENTRUY	DIFFERENCE IN HEIGHT
	CLIMB 560 M, DESCENT 630 M

4.4% ALCOHOL CONTENT

DOUBLE YEAST-FERMENTATION

 BLONDE

 STRAWBERRY ELDERBERRY RASPBERRY

 FULL-BODIED HARMONIOUS

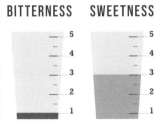

BITTERNESS   SWEETNESS

DESCRIPTION OF THE JOURNEY

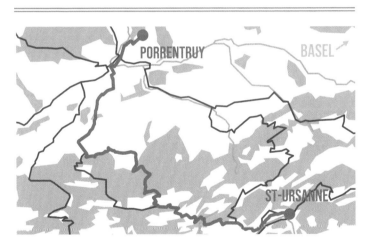

St-Ursanne (491m) → Seleute → Pt. 848
→ Vacherie Mouillard → Villars → Dô lai Tieudre
→ Champs Graitoux → Porrentruy (424m)

St-Ursanne is on the railroad line Delémont-Delle.

The station is far above the town. So, go downhill diagonally towards the center of St-Ursanne. This will allow you to catch an occasional glimpse of the town and the Doubs River. You enter the old part of town through an entrance cut into a tower (Porte Sainte-Pierre).

Stroll through the streets or go directly to the Porte Saint-Paul which is near the signpost for the walk. The third gate (Porte Saint-Jean) leads to a bridge on the Doubs River offering a lovely view of the town. From the Porte Saint-Jean, follow the marked path in the direction of Oisonfontaine-Seleute. You will soon leave the road, climbing slightly to the right towards the mountain. You will quickly have a beautiful view of the Clos du Doubs.

Some short portions of the forest trail toward Oisonfontaine require sure footing. Once you're in front of Seleute, at the edge of the forest, a hiking sign indicates to go right. That's the path to take. Be careful because there is another sign on a telephone pole a few meters farther.

In Seleute, follow the marked path in the direction of Les Chainions, until pt. 848 near the high-voltage line. From there, continue on the same path towards Porrentruy via Villars. When going down to Vacherie Mouillard, you will see the Vosges. From the Vacherie, Porrentruy is no longer indicated on the sign. Simply continue your descent towards Villars via the forest. From the edge of this forest you will see Porrentruy Castle.

From Villars, the marked path in the direction of Féteux passes near the recreation area Dô lai Tieudre. Follow the path until the next fork, where you will follow the direction of Porrentruy.

The path goes through fields and you arrive in the town near a school. In the old part of town, the marked path passes in front of the tourist office where you could once buy the homemade beer of Porrentruy. This is no longer the case. But if you ask, someone can certainly tell where to find it. You can often buy it at the minimarket Pam, which is a few meters farther down the street going towards the station, in an arcade to the left.

If it's out of stock at the minimarket, you can find it at the shop Les Vergers d'Ajoie. To go there, follow the marked path until the station and continue to follow it in the direction of Sur Le Mont. The path leads to the edge of the forest via an underground passage. There, leave the marked path and go up the staircase until you reach a street. Take a right towards the chapel. After the chapel, climb to the left via the Rue de Lorette, which is first paved and then changes into a forest path, until you reach the shop Les Vergers d'Ajoie, where you can buy the homemade beer of Porrentruy, as well as other local products. The round trip from the station to the shop takes 40 minutes, which is not included in the walk indicated above.

SHORTCUT

A bus service runs from Villars to Porrentruy (less often on weekends). You can therefore shorten the walk by an hour and a half.

RETURN

Porrentruy is on the railroad line Delle-Delémont.

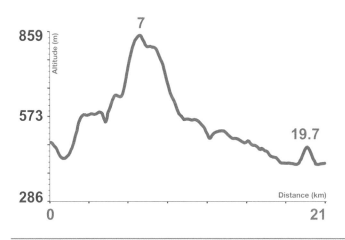

BRASSERIE ARTISANALE DE PORRENTRUY
Route de Courgenay 86
2900 Porrentruy
078 718 51 66
http://sites.google.com/site/
brasserieporrentruy

JURA TOURISME
Rue de la Gruère
62350 Saignelégier
+41 32 432 41 60
info@juratourisme.ch
www.j3l.ch

RUE P. PÉQUIGNAT 7
2900 Porrentruy
032 466 24 60

LES VERGERS D'AJOIE
Combe Druequelin 27
2900 Porrentruy
032 466 80 03
www.lesvergersdajoie.ch

ALLSCHWIL

A WALK RICH IN ENTERTAINMENT IN THE DIRECTION OF BASEL

BL

STARTING POINT	**DESTINATION**
# SCHÖNENBUCH	## PIER ON THE PORT OF BASEL
BEER	**DIFFICULTY**
## UNSER BIER	## WALK (WITH NARROW PATHS FOR A SHORT DISTANCE)
MAP	
## SHEET 213	**LENGTH OF THE WALK**
## (BASEL)	# 2H15, 10KM
INTERESTING SIGHT	**DIFFERENCE IN HEIGHT**
## HALF-TIMBERED HOUSES IN ALLSCHWIL	CLIMB 40 M DESCENT 150 M

4% ALCOHOL CONTENT	NON-FILTERED NATURALLY CLOUDY AND BOTTOM-FERMENTED

 STRAW-COLORED

 FRUITY

 LIGHT

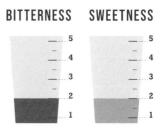

BITTERNESS SWEETNESS

DESCRIPTION OF THE JOURNEY

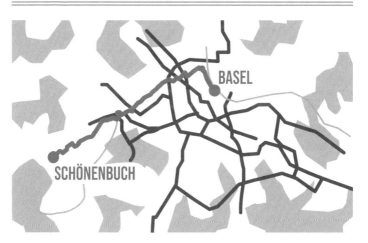

Schönenbuch (360 m) → Allschwil → Basel (244 m)

Take the trail leading through Allschwil in the direction of Kannenfeldplatz to Basel. This is the shortest version of the walk which goes through Ziegelschür. This path first leads to the edge of a forest and then follows the Lützelbach River through the old village of Allschwil, where you can admire the traditional Sundgau-style half-timbered houses. Next, walk about 500 meters along the main road (very busy).

From there, the path goes along a dirt embankment under the shade of trees. After about two kilometers, the river disappears under the ground. Take a stroll down a few of the local streets until you reach Kannenfeld Park. Cross the park, which has hundred-year-old trees, and then turn right to arrive at Kannenfeldplatz. Here you will find a footpath sign indicating Schönenbuch as the direction from where you just came, which is correct. In the opposite direction, "Wanderweg" is the only thing written. That's the path that you take to reach the Rhine River by St. Johanns Park. Turn right and follow the bank of the river upstream. This very wide river is often full of life with its waterfowl and the passage of cargo ships. At the second bridge, you must climb up the steps to get to the bus and tram stop Schifflände. Unfortunately the Lällekönig restaurant, which was the original end of this hike and had lots of Basel beers on tap, has closed down. Luckily there are many other restaurants in Basel's old town that serve Unser Bier. Check out the Unser Bier website for an up-to-date list.

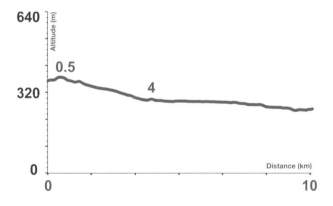

RETURN

Tram number 11 in the direction of Basel SBB.

BRAUEREI UNSER BIER
Gundeldingerstr. 287
4053 Basel
061 338 83 83
www.unser-bier.ch

INTERESTING SIGHTS
*   Half-timbered houses in Allschwil
*   Kannenfeld Park, the biggest park in Basel, with diverse vegetation.

ALP SIGEL

A MOUNTAINOUS RAMPART IN THE APPENZELL REGION

AI

STARTING POINT	**DESTINATION**
# SCHWENDE	# WASSERAUEN
BEER	**DIFFICULTY**
QUÖLLFRISCH	ALPINE HIKE
MAP	
SHEET 227	**LENGTH OF THE ALPINE HIKE**
(APPENZELL)	# 4H15, 9KM
INTERESTING SIGHT	**DIFFERENCE IN HEIGHT**
THE COLORFUL FAÇADE OF THE HOTEL ALPENROSE	CLIMB 870 M DESCENT 840 M

BLONDE
NON-FILTERED
NATURALLY
CLOUDY

 GOLDEN
YELLOW

 FRESH

 FULL-BODIED
AND MALTY

BITTERNESS   SWEETNESS

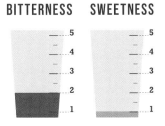

DESCRIPTION OF THE JOURNEY

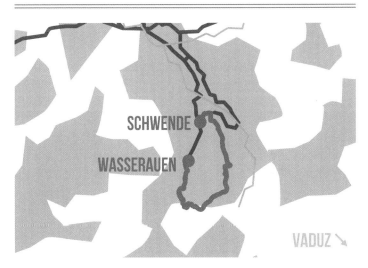

Schwende (842 m) → Zahme Gocht (1662 m)
→ Alp Sigel → Wasserauen (872m)

You can reach Swchende by train on the Appenzeller
line (Appenzellerbahn) from Gossau or Appenzell. The
stop is by request only, so don't forget to push the
button. Once you arrive at the station of Schwende,
follow the hiking trail in the direction of Zahme Gocht-
Alp Sigel. The trail leads to a steep path crossing a

ridge under a cliff. The path winds through the high mountain pasture of Bärstein and ends at the foot of the cliff.

You quickly gain altitude thanks to the path's steep slope. A crevasse makes it possible to climb the vertical wall. The path is clearly visible and secured by metal cables. You suddenly arrive on a small plateau with a magnificent view of the entire Alpstein massif and well beyond, all the way to Lake Constance. It takes 15 minutes to get to the mountain hut of Alp Sigel. Here, turn right on the path which goes in the direction of Mans-Wasserauen. Continue on this path, which is practically flat, crossing meadows and a lovely forest to get to Alp Mans. The descent to Wasserauen is very steep but easy enough as the trail is in good condition. At the end, this trail leads across a ravine where you can see beautiful waterfalls and wonderful rock formations.

The trail forks a little before Wasserauen. You can descend straight on until the hotel Alpenrose or descend diagonally until the station to reach the Gartenrestaurant. Both places serve locally brewed Appenzell Quöllfrisch beer.

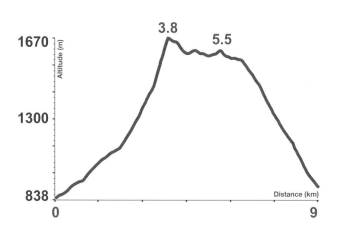

RETURN

From Wasserauen, take the Appenzellerbahn (AB train) in the direction of Appenzell and Gossau.

GASTHAUS ALPENROSE (THE ROSE OF THE ALPS)
9057 Wasserauen
071 799 11 33
www.alpenrose-ai.ch

GARTENRESTAURANT
Bahnhof Wasserauen

APPENZELLER BIER
Brauerei Locher AG
Brauereiplatz 1
9050 Appenzell
071 788 01 40
www.appenzellerbier.ch

INTERESTING SIGHTS
· The painted facade of the hotel Alpenrose, The Rose of the Alps.

AREUSE

ON THE TRAIL OF A DRAGON

NE

STARTING POINT	DESTINATION
NOIRAIGUE	**CORTAILLOD**

BEER	DIFFICULTY
LA VOUIVRE VERTE	**WALK**

MAP

SHEET 241
(VAL DE TRAVERS)

SHEET 242
(AVENCHE)

LENGTH OF THE WALK

4H, 16KM

INTERESTING SIGHT

SAUT DE BROT
THE MINERAL SPACE

DIFFERENCE IN HEIGHT

CLIMB 120 M
DESCENT 410 M

5.5% ALCOHOL CONTENT

BLONDE
NON-FILTERED
AND BOTTOM-
FERMENTED

 COPPERY

 FLORAL

 HOPPED

BITTERNESS

SWEETNESS

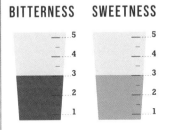

DESCRIPTION OF THE JOURNEY

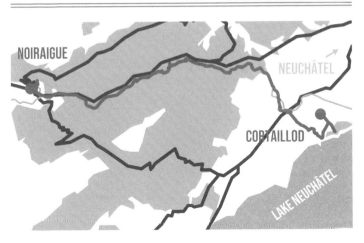

Noiraigue (728m) → Champ du Moulin → Boudry
→ Cortaillod (429m)

La Vouivre beer is named after a dragon that is said to
have lived at the source of the Areuse River.

Noiraigue is on the railroad line Neuchâtel-Buttes. You
can find a shop with local specialties right in the station,
as well the tourist office of Val de Travers.
From the station in Noiraigue, don't take the marked trail
in the direction Gorges de l'Areuse (Areuse Gorges), but
walk in the direction of Les Emposieux by taking the street

rue du Temple until a four-street intersection. There, cross the street rue du Pont until the street rue de la Source. Then, take a left (brown signpost "Source"). At the end of this street you see the karstic source of Noiraigue. Its water comes from a river which disappears near Les Ponts-de-Martel and flows underground for four kilometers. Return to the same trail at the four-street intersection. Take a left (brown signpost La Ferme Robert) and walk to the railroad platform. Next, follow the path marked Gorges de l'Areuse towards Boudry.

The upper part of the path is paved in places, but it is most often covered with gravel with natural stone steps or wooden footbridges. In the narrowest places of the gorges, it is dug directly into the rock. A number of bridges cross over the river. From time to time you pass in front of an old power plant. At times, the Areuse flows gently along a wide bed, but it roars in the waterfalls and the rapids, surrounded by high rock walls.

There are lots of things to see on the way. Le Saut de Brot bubbles at the bottom of a crevice. Just before le Champ du Moulin (The Field Mill), la Maison de la Nature has exhibitions of the local flora and fauna.

Next, you pass in front of l'Espace Minéral (The Mineral Space), where you can admire and buy fossils from the area. At the signpost Autres Directions (Other Directions) at Champ du Moulin, take the time to look behind you. The sight of le Creux du Van is well worth it. Further along your descent, make a detour via la Chute de la Verrière. In the lower part of the gorge you can see la Baume du Four on the left slope of the trail, a cavern in which objects from the Stone Age were found.

At the end of the gorge, you pass under a railroad viaduct. After about five minutes in the direction of Boudry TN, near a bridge, the trail branches off to the right towards the Castle of Boudry (brown sign). At the sign, leave the marked path to get to the castle which houses the Museum of Wine. Shortly beyond the castle, you will enter the city gate in order to cross the old town of Boudry. At the end of the old town there is a yellow sign (without writing). There, take a right and go under a street. Then, zigzag up via a small forest. Once at the top, cross the industrial park of Cortaillod until you reach the heart of the old village. From Cortaillod, follow the trail in the direction of La Tuilière via Rebberge while going down towards Petit Cortaillod.

There are three ways to drink La Vouivre. If the brewery is open, follow le Sentier du Lac for ten minutes until the white sign indicating this brewery (about 250 m). You can also find it at the hotel le Vaisseau, in Petit Cortaillod and at the restaurant Buffet d'un Tram. To get to Buffet d'un Tram, take le Sentier du Lac from Petit Cortaillod until you come to a fork, then follow the marked path in the direction of Areuse Tram.

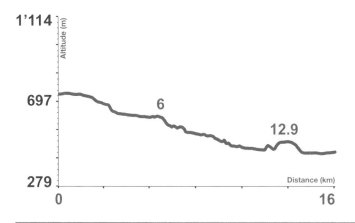

RETURN

Petit Cortaillod: In summertime, you can take a boat from "Petit Cortaillod" to Nauchâtel (but not every day), or you can go to the restaurant Buffet d'un Tram (15 minutes), as indicated above.

Brasserie: Brewery: From the brewery, return to the white sign and the "Cortaillod Câbles" bus stop is only a few steps to your right. A bus (not many) will take you to Areuse Littorail or to the stop Cortaillod Bas-de-Sachet, with a connection to Areuse Littorail. Or you can continue straight on from the sign towards the restaurant Buffet d'un Tram (15 minutes from the brewery).

Buffet d'un Tram: From this restaurant, go to the bus stop Bas-de-Sachet (100 m), which has many buses every hour going to Areuse Littorail, a stop that is on the tram line Boudry-Neuchâtel Place Pury. Several buses link Place Pury to the station in Neuchâtel.

BRASSERIE LA VOUIVRE
la Tertillière 5
2016 Cortaillod
079 374 08 10
www.brasserie-lavouivre.ch

RESTAURANT LE BUFFET D'UN TRAM
avenue François-Borel 3
2016 Cortaillod
032 842 29 92
www.buffetduntram.ch

RESTAURANT LE VAISSEAU
Place Marcel de Coulon
2016 Cortaillod
032 843 44 77
www.hotel-le-vaisseau.ch

MAISON DE LA NATURE NEUCHÂTELOISE
2149 Champ-du-Moulin
032 853 38 45
www.maisonnaturene.ch

ESPACE MINÉRAL
Champ du Moulin
079 760 34 06

BABENTAL

SH

STARTING POINT	DESTINATION
OBERHALLAU	**SCHLEITHEIM**

BEER	DIFFICULTY
EIDGENOSS	**HIKE**

MAP	
SHEET 405	LENGTH OF THE HIKE
SCHAFFHAUSEN STEIN AM RHEIN	**3H15, 12KM**

INTERESTING SIGHT	DIFFERENCE IN HEIGHT
A NICELY DECORATED BUS SHELTER	CLIMB 310 M DESCENT 270 M

5.2% ALCOHOL CONTENT

NATURALLY CLOUDY BOTTOM-FERMENTED

 AMBER

 HINT OF MALT

 SWEET

BITTERNESS

5
4
3
2
1

SWEETNESS

5
4
3
2
1

DESCRIPTION OF THE JOURNEY

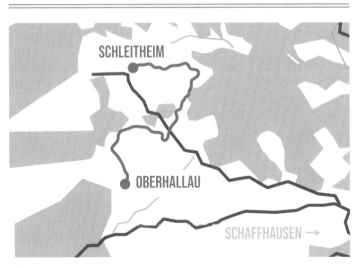

SCHLEITHEIM

OBERHALLAU

SCHAFFHAUSEN →

Oberhallau (434 m) → Hammel (615 m)
→ Siblingerhöhe → Babental → Schleitheim (470 m)

You can get to Oberhallau by bus from Schaffhausen and Neunkirch.

When you reach the Oberhallau bus stop, you will see only one hiking sign showing "Wanderweg" in both directions.

There is, however, another sign close to the church. From there, follow the path towards Hinter Berghöf. The track goes through the imposing Winzerdorf and continues through the vineyards towards Hinter Berghöf on the Oberhallauberg.

At this point, take the hiking path in the direction of Siblingerhöhe. Just after that, you can leave the road. If the corn is not too high, you have a fabulous view of the Alps.

When you get up to Siblingerhöhe, cross the street and follow the hiking path towards Babental. The path will lead you through a mixed forest at the foot of Lang Randen. In spring, you can find wild garlic here. The Babental is the one and only mountain pasture in the canton of Schaffhausen. In addition, there is a bistro where you can enjoy a Falken beer. You will need two and a quarter hours to reach this point. Interestingly enough, the first collective agreement in Switzerland was signed between the Falken brewery and the labor unions in 1886.

From Babental, follow the hiking trail that leads to Schleitheim. This path offers a wide panorama, with huge fields as far as the eye can see. In Schleitheim, stay on the hiking path until you see a pedestrian bridge on the right-hand side, after the Alder bus stop.

Cross the bridge and walk to the post office. All the buses stop here. It is roughly a one-hour walk from Babental to the post office.

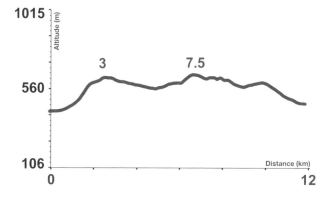

RETURN

By post bus to Schaffhausen via Siblingerhöhe.

ALP-RESTAURANT BABENTAL
052 680 12 72
www.babental.ch

BRAUEREI FALKEN
Brauereistrasse 1
8201 Schaffhausen
052 632 00 00
www.falken.ch

INTERESTING SIGHTS
*   A nicely decorated bus shelter in Siblingerhöhe
*   The enclosure for small animals in Babental

BALDERN

FROM THE SAULIAMT INTO THE CITY

ZH

STARTING POINT	DESTINATION
LAKE TÜRLER	**ZURICH**

BEER	DIFFICULTY
REKORD	**HIKE**

MAP	
SHEET 225	LENGTH OF THE HIKE
(ZURICH)	**4H30, 17KM**

INTERESTING SIGHT	DIFFERENCE IN HEIGHT
THE PLANET PATH	CLIMB 400 M DESCENT 550 M

5.2% ALCOHOL CONTENT

BROWN
NON-FILTERED
NATURALLY
CLOUDY

 AMBER

 FRUITY

 MALTY

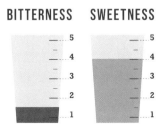

BITTERNESS   SWEETNESS

DESCRIPTION OF THE JOURNEY

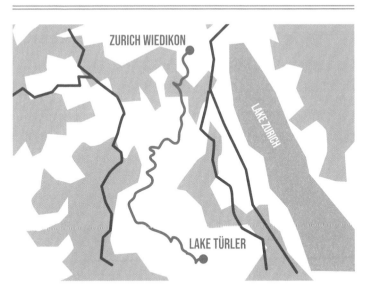

Lake Türler (643 m) → Müliberg → Dachs
→ Dürrenbach → Ägerten → Balderen
→ Annaburg (800 m) → Albisgüetli → Panoramaweg
→ Zurich Wiedikon (460 m)

The Türlersee bus stop is on the Zurich-Wiedikon /
Hausen am Albis bus line. At the stop, follow the
circular path of Türlersee.

The lake is a few minutes away. Turn right and follow the north-east bank to the northern end of the lake. From there, follow the road for Müliberg. Go through this village in order to get to the rest area in Dachs. Then, follow the road towards Dürrenbach. This path goes along the forest until the street linking Sennweid to Eggmatt. Here, you will come to a sign indicating Dürrenbach. It's about 500 meters south of the farm of Dürrenbach. Leave the trail and continue straight on. After about 400 meters you get to a street on the road to Wetswill ("Wanderweg" is the only indication). Turn right and make your way to the forest's edge. Follow the edge of the forest, which overlooks a small marsh, until you get to the next sign, about 20 minutes away. Continue towards Wettswil.

You'll see a large stone on the edge of the trail. Still going along the edge of the forest, you pass in front of a firing range. Ignore the second circular path and continue to follow the sign "Wanderweg." You will walk past a nice little pond in the forest then come to a fork just before Bonstetten. There, take the path via Ägerten in the direction of Balderen and continue your descent until you reach the "Ägerten" bus stop in Reppischtal. At this spot, cross the street and climb the slope in the direction of Balderen. In Balderen, follow the "Planetenweg," direction Uetliberg. Just after the Uto Staffel restaurant the downward road forks in the direction of Albisgüetli. It separates very quickly into two. To the right, you will see a ridge path marked in yellow, less steep than the other, from which the highway is often visible and noisy. To the left, the Laternenweg is steeper but quieter because the highway is hidden.

Further down, the two paths meet up. Ignore the sign Leimbach and continue following the sign "Wanderweg." Walk roughly 200 meters along the edge of the forest until you reach the tram station Albisgüetli. Unfortunately, the original goal of this hike, the restaurant Schweighof, has closed down. You can find Turnbinen beer at many restaurants and bars in Zurich, however there's unfortunately no list on the brewery's website.

To get to the brewery itself, take tram 13 to Paradeplatz, change to tram 2 heading towards Farbhof until you reach the Freihofstrasse stop. From there, walk in the same direction that the tram was travelling in until you reach the Turbinen brewery at Badenerstrasse 571.

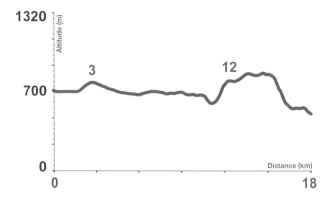

SHORTCUT

Instead of taking the post bus all the way to Türlersee, get off at Aegerten and do only the second part of the hike. It should only last about two hours.

RETURN

The easiest, though longest route from the brewery back to Zurich main station is to take the tram 2 to Stauffacher, then change to tram 3 or 14, both of which go to the station. It'll take about 25 minutes.

TURBINEN-BRÄU
Badenerstr. 571
8048 Zurich
044 440 54 14
www.turbinenbraeu.ch

INTERESTING SIGHTS
*   Lake Türler
    (Türlersee)
*   The Planet Path
    (Planetenweg)

BRUDERHOLZ

FROM A VACATION RESORT AREA TO THE OLD CITY OF BASEL

BL

STARTING POINT	**DESTINATION**
# ETTINGEN	# BASEL
BEER	**DIFFICULTY**
UELI BIER	
MAP	**HIKE**
SHEET 213	**LENGTH OF THE HIKE**
(BASEL)	# 3H15, 15KM
INTERESTING SIGHT	**DIFFERENCE IN HEIGHT**
BASEL ZOO	CLIMB 200 M DESCENT 270 M

5.4% ALCOHOL CONTENT

BLONDE
NATURALLY
CLOUDY TOP-
FERMENTED

 GOLDEN
YELLOW

 FRUITY

 CLOVE

BITTERNESS	SWEETNESS
5	5
4	4
3	3
2	2
1	1

DESCRIPTION OF THE JOURNEY

BASEL

ETTINGEN

Ettingen (329 m) → Bottmingen → Basel (244 m)

You can get to Ettingen by tram number 10 from the main station in Basel.

Follow the footpath in the direction of Basel / St. Margarethen. After the last houses when leaving Ettingen, you arrive at a vast plain. Walk through the forest leading to Bruderholz.
At the second intersection after the edge of the forest (to the left of the letter "d" of Bruderholz on the map

1 / 50,000), the signpost points in the wrong direction.
Don't go left. Instead, continue straight on. You will
have have many opportunities to admire the
magnificent landscape of the Black Forest and the
Vosges.

In Bottmingen, go down a slight slope and pass
through a residential neighborhood.

When the road starts to slope upward, turn left. The
yellow hiking signpost is hidden behind some white
signs for wheelchair trails. Soon after, turn right and
you can admire a wonderful view, this time of the city
of Basel.

At the Margarethen tram stop, continue on the
Jubiläumsweg (on the Pruntruterstrasse).

You pass the Zoo tram stop to arrive at the Birsig
River. Next, go through the old city until you reach the
pier. From there, continue along the Erasmus
Stadtrundgang (a circular city walk). The way is
indicated by a red sign with a head and a red arrow.
Follow this itinerary and continue on the Rheinsprung
(which is an avenue) until the cathedral. Just before
the cathedral, turn left towards the Pfalz, where you
can once again admire the Rhine River.

Next, take the staircase down to the ferry and enjoy a
quiet ride across the Rhine River. On the other side,
walk a few meters along the river until you reach
Referenzgässlein, which allows you to get to the
Rheingasse. There you'll find the Fischerstube brewery
and restaurant, where they brew and sell Ueli Beer.

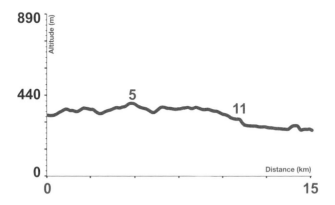

RETURN

When leaving Fischerstube, take a right onto the avenue Rheingasse until the tram stop Rheingasse and continue with tram number 8 until the Basel main station (SBB).

UELI BIER
Brauerei und Restaurant Fischerstube
Rheingasse 45
4058 Basel
061 692 92 00
www.restaurant-fischerstube.ch
www.uelibier.ch

INTERESTING SIGHTS
*   Basel Zoo
    www.zoobasel.ch
*   Ferry ride on the Rhine River
    www.faehri.ch

BUCHEGGBERG

A SMALL SANDSTONE MOUNTAIN

SO

STARTING POINT	DESTINATION
LOHN-LÜTERKOFEN	**AETIGKOFEN**
BEER	DIFFICULTY
BUECHIBÄRGER	**HIKE**
MAP	
SHEET 233	LENGTH OF THE HIKE
(SOLOTHURN)	**2H30, 10KM**
INTERESTING SIGHT	DIFFERENCE IN HEIGHT
SANDSTONE CAVE	CLIMB 300 M DESCENT 150 M

4.8% ALCOHOL CONTENT

BLONDE
NON-FILTERED
NATURALLY
CLOUDY

 YELLOW

 SWEET

 SWEET

BITTERNESS SWEETNESS

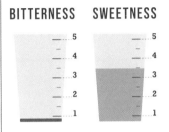

DESCRIPTION OF THE JOURNEY

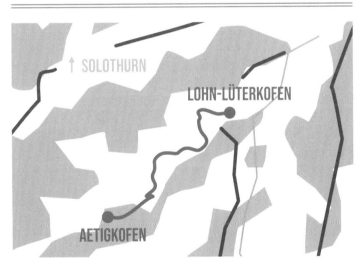

Station Lohn-Lüterkofen (464 m) → Lüterkofen
→ Küttigkofen → Mülital → Wolftürli → Aetigkofen (610 m)

The brochure concerning the third forest hike in
Solothurn can be ordered by calling 032 627 23 41.

Lohn-Lüterkofen is on the Bern RBS – Solothurn train
line. The company RBS has its own small station in the
central station of Bern.

You get to it by taking the underground passage toward the Neuengasse exit.

From the Lohn-Lüterkofen station, follow the hiking trail in the direction of Küttigkofen. Follow the Biberenbach stream to Lüterkofen, then climb to the top of the Höchi for an unrestricted view of the Alps. From Küttigkofffen, walk along the Mülibach in the direction of Buchegg. Just before pt. 494, the trail turns to the left and passes in front of a house.

After this house, leave the hiking trail that goes to Buchegg and turn right. Take the third forest trail in Solothurn crossing the Mülital. The signpost is hard to see. The path winds along the Mülibach via a narrow and wild valley. In the sandstone cliff, there is a small cave followed by a spring a little farther along. All these natural beauties, and others, are described on the information signs. Shortly before pt. 9, take the shortcut that passes through Brügeln, which will take you back to the forest trail between pts. 26 and 27. This shortcut is indicated in the brochure, but it isn't indicated on the path.

Take a small paved street that goes to the left a few meters before pt. 9. This narrow and climbing road takes you to the forest. At the edge of the forest the road stops and the road branches off in three directions. Take the one in the middle. It gently climbs and follows a big arc that runs into the third forest trail of Solothurn. Here, turn right in the direction of pt. 26. When you arrive at Wolftürli, a little after pt. 24, leave the forest trail of Solothurn. Turn right onto the path which goes in the direction of Aetigkofen. From the edge of the forest, there is a clear view of Weissenstein, Hasenmatt and Grenchenberg. After crossing a small part of the forest, you will overlook the village of Aetigkofen. In the center of the village at the restaurant Bären you can drink Buechibärger Bier either under the pergola or in the dining room, which is arranged very nicely.

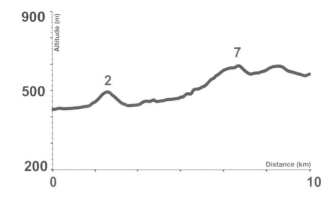

RETURN

Follow the hiking path for another 5 minutes until the post bus stop Aetigkofen. From here you can take the post bus to Lohn-Lüterkofen. There aren't many post buses, especially during the weekend.

RESTAURANT BÄREN
Britternstrasse 11
4583 Aetigkofen/SO
032 661 10 69

BUECHIBÄRGER BIER
079 444 76 20
079 730 39 76
www.buechibaergerbier.ch

INTERESTING SIGHTS
- Sandstone cave
- A spring
- Several beech tree forests

CHASSERAL

THROUGH A NARROW GORGE TO THE EXPANSES OF THE JURA

BE

STARTING POINT	DESTINATION
VILLERET	**COURTELARY**

BEER	DIFFICULTY
ALBERTUS	**ALPINE HIKE**

MAP	
SHEET 232	LENGTH OF THE ALPINE HIKE
(ST-IMIER VALLEY)	**6H, 17KM**

INTERESTING SIGHTS	DIFFERENCE IN HEIGHT
THE COMBE GREDE A GORGE	CLIMB 930 M DESCENT 980 M

5.2% ALCOHOL CONTENT

BLONDE
FILTERED
BOTTOM-
FERMENTED

 PALE GOLD

 HONEY

 GRAINY

BITTERNESS   SWEETNESS

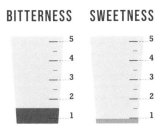

DESCRIPTION OF THE JOURNEY

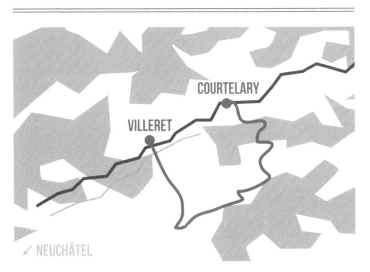

Villeret (763 m) → Combe Grède → Chasseral (1607 m)
→ La Neuve → Métairie du Milieu de Bienne
→ Petite Douanne → Courtelary (701 m)

Villeret is on the train line between Bienne and La
Chaux-de-Fonds.

The path that goes through Combe Grède is very well
laid-out and maintained. You need to be surefooted

though. The stones are often wet and a little slippery. If it is snowy or icy, the path becomes dangerous. You cannot completely exclude the risk of falling rocks. As you must use ladders to climb over some boulders, this hike is not suitable for dogs.

From the station of Villeret, you can already see the gorge that leads straight to Chasseral through the woods. Follow the hiking path towards Combe Grède-Chasseral, which takes you from the edge of the village to the gorge. At the beginning, the path is quite flat, and then it becomes steeper and has cliffs that are almost vertical on both sides. As you walk, you can marvel at the different rock layers and eddies.

In Pré aux Auges, next to a rest area before a fountain, you leave the gorge. Shortly after the rest area, you can choose between two routes to get to Chasseral. Turn right at this crossroads. Go across a small valley and climb up a steep path to reach the ridge where the Chasseral Hotel stands. This ridge offers a clear view of the Alps and the three lakes of the Jura. The hotel serves La 1607 beer, brewed specially by the brewery Bieres & Co. for the restaurant at 1607 meters above sea level.

From there, continue along the Métairie du Milieu de Bienne path. This runs along the Chasseral / Signal ridge and leads directly to the radio tower. Walk for another good kilometer and turn left to leave the ridge.

You will reach the Métairie du Milieu de Bienne after crossing La Neuve. In this comfortable "Alpbeizli" you can find beer from the Egger brewery. From Métairie, head downhill in the direction of Courtelary via Petite Douanne. The path in the meadows is not always easy to see. As there is sometimes quite a distance between two signposts, it's worth checking the map from time to time.

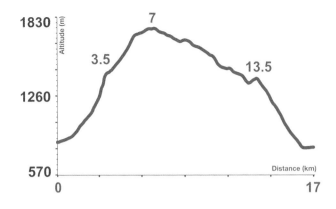

RETURN

Courtelary is on the train line between Bienne and La Chaux-de-Fonds.

HÔTEL CHASSERAL
032 751 24 51
www.chasseral-hotel.ch

MÉTAIRIE DU MILIEU DE BIENNE
032 943 10 34

EGGER BIER
Brauereiweg 3
3076 Worb
031 838 14 14
www.eggerbier.ch

INTERESTING SIGHTS
· La Combe Grède, a gorge

CHRÜZHUBEL

BETWEEN PILATUS AND ENTLEBUCH

LU

STARTING POINT	**DESTINATION**
# MALTERS	# LUCERNE
BEER	**DIFFICULTY**
## LUZERNER BIER	
MAP	## HIKE
## SHEET 235	**LENGTH OF THE HIKE**
## (ROTKREUZ)	# 4H45, 15KM
INTERESTING SIGHT	**DIFFERENCE IN HEIGHT**
## RÄNGGLOCH	**CLIMB 790 M**
A GORGE	**DESCENT 840 M**

5.0% ALCOHOL CONTENT

NON-FILTERED NATURALLY CLOUDY AND BOTTOM-FERMENTED

 GOLDEN YELLOW

 HOPPED

 DELICATE

BITTERNESS   SWEETNESS

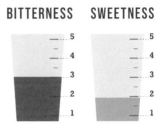

DESCRIPTION OF THE JOURNEY

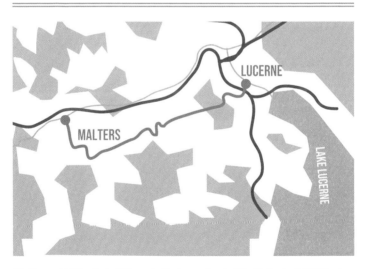

Malters (496 m) → Siten → Scharmis → Chrüzhubel (998 m) →Ränggloch → Sonnenberg (800 m) → Gütschwald → Gütsch → Luzern (436 m)

Malters is on the railroad line between Lucerne and Bern, which also passes through Entlebuch.

From the station, follow the footpath in the direction of Siten (marked as Site on the map). Shortly afterwards, the path rises and runs alongside a stream before crossing meadows and a forest. From Siten, do not head directly for Lucerne but go through a forest and continue on a small plateau in the direction of Scharmis.

From there, follow the path through the Chrüzhubel in the direction of Lucerne. It takes you up onto a ridge of the Blattenberg mountain. On the right-hand side you have an unrestricted view of Mount Pilatus, and on the left-hand side you can look out over the plateau as far as the eye can see.

When you reach the very end of the ridge, walk down towards Ränggloch. Here, the Ränggbach (a river) has carved out a narrow and deep gorge on its way towards Kleinen Emme. First, cross the Ränggbach and a little further on cross over a very busy street. Then, climb back up in the direction of Sonnenberg, crossing the Chrüzhöchi.

As soon as you leave the forest, you have a magnificent view over Lake Lucerne (also known as the Four-Cantons Lake).

The arrival station for the Sonnenbergbahn funicular railway is in the center of Lucerne's recreation area. You will have access to many hiking and walking trails, as well as two restaurants. Take the trail towards Bruchmatt-Luzern and follow this path until you get to a crossroads which turns left in the direction of Gütschwald. At the next signpost (pt. 528), turn right towards Gütsch.

You can get down to Lucerne either on foot or on the Gütsch funicular railway. Both options offer marvelous views of the town and the mountains.

Next to the station, the footpath leads to a stairway leading down to Lucerne. The path leads directly to the Reuss via the Geissmattbrücke. There, turn right and follow the Reuss until you reach the train station. You can drink Luzerner Bier in several of the town's restaurants. The brewery's website has an up-to-date list of these restaurants.

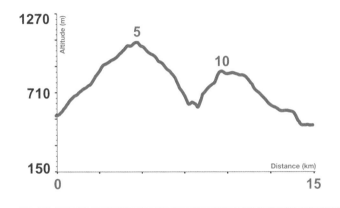

RESTAURANT SCHWYZERHÜSLI
Sonnenberg
041 320 21 31
www.schwyzerhuesli.net

HOTEL SONNENBERG
041 320 66 44
www.hotelsonnenberg.ch

LUZERNER BIER
Bürgenstrasse 16
6005 Luzern
041 252 00 52
www.brauerei.lu

INTERESTING SIGHTS
· Ränggloch, a gorge
· Sonnenbergbahn, the old funicular railway
  www.erlebnis-sonnenberg.ch

DOUBS

ON THE BANKS OF THE RIVER AND ACROSS THE DENSE FOREST
OF THE FRANCHES-MONTAGNES

JU

STARTING POINT	DESTINATION
LE NOIRMONT	**SAIGNELÉGIER**
BEER	DIFFICULTY
LA SALAMANDRE	
MAP	**ALPINE HIKE**
SHEET 222	
(CLOS DU DOUBS)	LENGTH OF THE ALPINE HIKE
	4H45, 15KM
INTERESTING SIGHT	DIFFERENCE IN HEIGHT
THE THEUSSERET NATURE RESERVE	CLIMB 690 M DESCENT 680 M

TOP-FERMENTED

 YELLOW

 SPICY, FRUITY

 REFRESHING

BITTERNESS   **SWEETNESS**

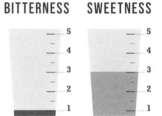

DESCRIPTION OF THE JOURNEY

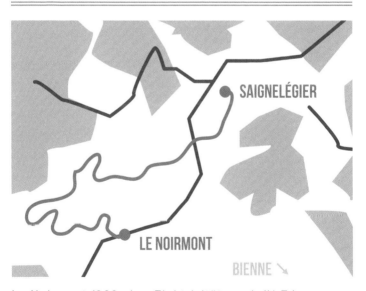

Le Noirmont (969 m) → Elektrizitätswerk (U.E.)
→ Doubs (500 m) → Le Theusseret → Chez le Bolé
→ Les Sommêtres (1079 m) → Muriaux
→ Saignelégier (982 m)

Le Noirmont is on the railroad line linking
La Chaux-de-Fonds to Tavannes.
Although this hike is indicated by yellow signs, the

climb from Le Theusseret to Chez le Bolé is a mountain trail that requires surefootedness.

From the station in Le Noirmont, follow the path that descends in the direction of La Goule and leads to the power plant on the Doubs River (U.E. map). The forest track is wide, but it has a lot of smooth, partially moss-covered stones and can be very slippery when wet. In the lower part you can see the rock faces which were once the banks of the Doubs. Shortly before the power plant, the trail becomes a paved road. There, turn right towards Le Theusseret. You will soon arrive back on a dirt path. Further down, you cross the Theusseret Nature Reserve, where the forest is ancient.

Next to the restaurant Le Theusseret, you can admire a waterfall which is particularly impressive, depending on the season. From the waterfall, walk a few meters upstream to start the climb.

Follow the hiking trail in the direction of Chez le Bolé, Muriaux. This trail requires surefootedness. The trickiest parts are secured with chains and two sections are equipped with ladders. After descending 200 meters, you reach a panoramic viewpoint with a bench after which the path becomes easier. It follows l'Arête des Sommetres until pt. 1075, where there is a rest area.

From there, take the time for a little detour and enjoy the view from the mountain hut.

From the rest area, descend in the direction of Muriaux and cross the bridge that passes over the road and the railroad tracks. Then, continue in the same direction to get to Saignelégier. The beer of the Brasserie des Franches-Montagnes (BFM) can be ordered in many restaurants in the town. A list of these restaurants can be found on the brewery's website.

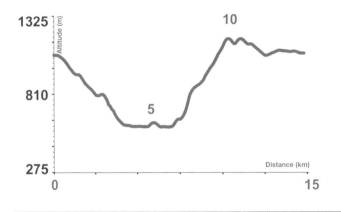

RESTAURANT LE THEUSSERET
032 951 14 51

BRASSERIE DES FRANCHES-MONTAGNES
chemin des Buissons 8
2350 Saignelégier/JU
032 951 26 26
www.brasseriebfm.ch

INTERESTING SIGHT
·   The Theusseret Nature Reserve, ancient forest

EETELWEIHER

FROM THE RHINE TO THE SURBTAL

AG

STARTING POINT	**DESTINATION**
# MELLIKON	# ENDINGEN
BEER	**DIFFICULTY**
KÜNDIG BRÄU	HIKE
MAP	
SHEET 215	**LENGTH OF THE HIKE**
(BADEN)	3H45, 14KM
INTERESTING SIGHT	**DIFFERENCE IN HEIGHT**
THE JEWISH HERITAGE PATH IN ENDINGEN	CLIMB 340 M DESCENT 300 M

5.0% ALCOHOL CONTENT

NON-FILTERED
NATURALLY
CLOUDY
TOP-FERMENTED

AMBER

FRESH

MALTY

KÜNDIG
BRÄU

BITTERNESS   SWEETNESS

5	5
4	4
3	3
2	2
1	1

DESCRIPTION OF THE JOURNEY

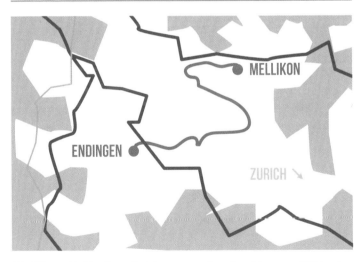

MELLIKON

ENDINGEN

ZURICH ↘

Mellikon (351 m) → Rekingen → An der Nurren (501 m)
→ Eetelweiher → Vogelsang → Endingen (386 m)

Mellikon is located on the train line between Eglisau
and Waldshut.

From the station, find your way to the Rhine River and
follow the riverbank until the station in Rekingen.
Starting the hike from Rekingen makes it 30 minutes

shorter. From Rekingen, climb to the viewpoint An der Nurren (indicated as Uf des Nurren on the signs). As soon as you leave the road and begin walking along the Rhine, the setting is very peaceful and quiet, except when the firing range in Chrüzlibachtal is being used. Fortunately, you can find information about upcoming shooting events at www.chruezlibach.ch. Shortly before the viewpoint Uf des Nurren, there is a yellow marker on a tree a few meters to the left of the forest trail. The path isn't easily seen, but it is marked further on. To get to the panoramic viewpoint, you will have to weave in and out of bushes and walk on roots. If you prefer an easier route, just stick to the forest trail and follow the yellow signposting to the left to reach the viewpoint. So, whether you're an adventurer or you prefer an easier path to get to the Uf der Nurren, everyone can enjoy the magnificent view over the Rhine River and the Black Forest. The look-out is equipped with benches and a grill.

From the viewpoint return to the last signpost and follow the trail along the ridge in the direction of Mülibach then continue following the path towards Endingen. It leads to Eetel-Weiher (Eetelweiher on the map), where the witch Etelwybli lived for hundreds of years. Next, cross the Althau while climbing a bit. From the forest's edge, there is a lovely view of the Jura.

While descending through the village of Vogelsang and passing in front of Hörndlihau in the direction of Endingen, you can see the Surbtal and the Ruckfeld, a truly vast plateau. In Endingen, cross the Surb in order to get to the main road. In front of the post bus stop, the Post restaurant serves locally brewed Kündig Bräu beer.

Endingen is the birthplace of Ruth Dreifuss, a former member of the Swiss Federal Council.

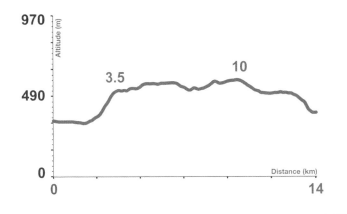

RETURN

From Endingen, buses run to Baden, Brugg, Niederweningen, Siggenthal-Würenlingen and Zurzach.

RESTAURANT POST
Marktgasse 18
5304 Endingen
056 242 10 80
www.restaurant-post-endingen.ch

KÜNDIG BRÄU
Hauptstrasse 30
5323 Rietheim AG
056 249 16 13
www.kuendigbrau.ch

INTERESTING SIGHT
* The Jewish Heritage Path in Endingen
  www.juedischerkulturweg.ch

ENTLISBERG

FROM THE SIHLTAL TO LAKE ZURICH

ZH

STARTING POINT	**DESTINATION**
LEIMBACH STATION	**ZURICH WOLLISHOFEN**
BEER	**DIFFICULTY**
AMBOSS AMBER	**HIKE**
MAP	
CITY MAP OF ZURICH	**LENGTH OF THE HIKE**
	1H30, 6KM
INTERESTING SIGHT	**DIFFERENCE IN HEIGHT**
ROTE FABRIK (RED FACTORY)	CLIMB 130 M DESCENT 160 M

BLONDE FILTERED AND BOTTOM-FERMENTED

 AMBER

 FLOWERY

 MALTY

BITTERNESS   **SWEETNESS**

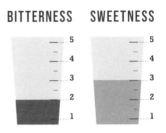

DESCRIPTION OF THE JOURNEY

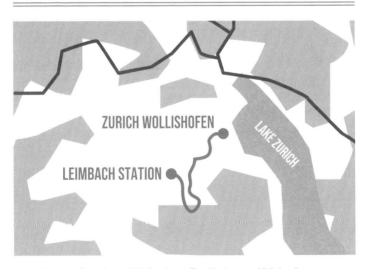

Leimbach Station (435 m) → Entlisberg (524 m)
→ Wollishofen (409 m)

You can get to Leimbach station by using the
Sihltalbahn, the railroad line of the Sihl.
The hiking signpost is located at the exit of the
underground passage. Do not go straight to
Wollishofen. First, follow the path that climbs the Sihl
in the direction of Adliswil until you reach the

southern end of Entlisberg. Here, the small wooded hill becomes mountainous. You can sometimes find rare plants growing on the steep slope which is surrounded by a pine tree forest and sandstone cliffs. When you arrive at the biotope with water lilies, frogs and dragonflies, turn left and follow the winding path leading up to Entlisbergchopf. Here, you will find a picnic area with fountains and grills.

From there, slowly continue the climb through the forest directly to Wollishofen. Occasional clearings between trees on your left allow you to admire a view of the Sihl Valley from the edge of the cliff.

Shortly after, you will come to the edge of the forest which dominates Wollishofen, where a relative stillness has once again settled. Previously, the highway split the leisure park of Entlisberg into two. The residents of the area had to fight for years against the highway and they were right to do so. The highway is now covered and the leisure park is once again accessible.

Take the Entlisbergstrasse and the Owen-weg to reach the tram stop Wollishofen. From there, you need to follow the path in the direction of Hirzel for about 250 meters before arriving at the street Kalchbüchlstrasse. Cross the street. Next, leave the hiking trail and continue straight on to the Honeggerweg. After about 200 meters, turn left onto the Eggpromenade. Follow this path, which has a splendid view of Lake Zurich, until the church in Wollishofen. To the right of the church, go down the pedestrian path leading to the Alte Kirche (signpost on the wall). Once at the Alte Kirche, take another right and walk down to the tram stop Post Wollishofen.

After crossing the Seestrasse, follow the hiking trail in the direction of Seeuferpromenade until the pier in Wollishofen. Turn to the right. Via a graveled road, you will arrive at the arts center Rote Fabrik (Red Factory), where the Ziegel oh Lac restaurant serves the beer Amboss.

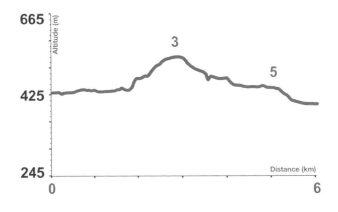

RETURN

Go back to the tram stop Post Wollishofen.
Take tram number 7 to get back to the main station of Zurich.

BEIZ ZIEGEL OH LAC
Seestrasse 407
8038 Zurich
044 481 62 42
www.ziegelohlac.ch

AMBOSS BIER
Zollstrasse 80
8005 Zurich
043 960 36 51
www.amboss-bier.ch

INTERESTING SIGHTS
* The covered highway
* The arts center Rote Fabrik (Red Factory)
  www.rotefabrik.ch

FANEZFURGGA

**FROM INCREDIBLE ROCK FORMATIONS TO
THE HIGHEST BREWERY IN EUROPE**

GR

STARTING POINT	DESTINATION
SERTIG SAND	**MONSTEIN**

BEER	DIFFICULTY
MONSTEINER HUUSBIER	**ALPINE HIKE**

MAP	
SHEET 258	LENGTH OF THE ALPINE HIKE
(BERGÜN/BRAVUOGN)	**5H, 14KM**

INTERESTING SIGHT	
THE WALSER HOUSES IN MONSTEIN	DIFFERENCE IN HEIGHT
	CLIMB 780 M DESCENT 1010 M

4.8% ALCOHOL CONTENT

NON-FILTERED NATURALLY CLOUDY AND BOTTOM-FERMENTED

 GOLDEN YELLOW

 SPICY

 MALTY

BITTERNESS   SWEETNESS

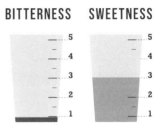

DESCRIPTION OF THE JOURNEY

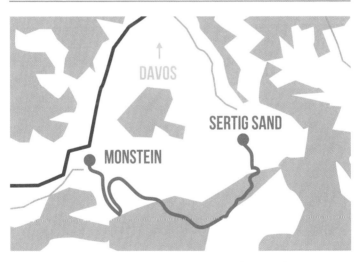

Sertig Sand (1859 m) → Fanezfurgga (2580 m)
→ Oberalp → Laubenalp → Monstein (1626 m)

You can get to Sertig Sand on the post bus that
leaves from Davos Platz.
The hiking signpost is not directly at the bus stop but
a short distance up the road. The path is well marked
and leads up the valley to a waterfall.
You will come to a steep section. After about half an

hour, you arrive at the top of the waterfall.
It is worth stopping here to take in the breathtaking
view of the village of Sertig down below. Then
continue your ascension through the valley.
Shortly afterwards, on both sides of the path, you can
admire impressive rocks of all shapes and colors.
Depending on the season, you can also see colorful
Alpine flowers. The path becomes steeper just before
the summit.
The Fanezfurgga descent leads you through a broad
valley until you reach Oberalp. From there you can go
straight down to Monstein and shorten the hike by
half an hour. Or you can turn left and go through a
beautiful mountain forest until you reach Laubenalp.
As the path has few uphill and downhill sections, it
almost follows a contour line.
From Laubenalp, take a small natural lane to
Monstein.
You can enjoy the Monsteiner Huusbier beer in the
Ducan hotel-restaurant, at the restaurant
"Veltlinerstübli" and, of course, directly at the
brewery. You can also buy it in the village shop.
Other local specialties are also available at the shop,
such as cheese, dried meat, and pasta.

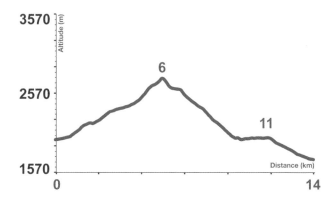

RETURN

From Monstein, you can take the post bus to Glaris station where there are links with the Rhaetian Railway or with the post buses for Davos and Lenzerheide. The trains only stop on request. Take care when preparing your itinerary: Monstein station is far down in the valley and there is no connecting service with the village above. For the post bus, be sure to use times scheduled for the village of Monstein.

HOTEL-RESTAURANT DUCAN
7278 Davos Monstein/GR
081 401 11 13
www.hotelducan.ch

RESTAURANT VELTLINERSTÜBLI
7278 Monstein/GR
081 401 11 52
www.veltlinerstuebli.ch

DORFLADEN
Haus zur Post
7278 Davos Monstein/GR
081 401 11 53

MONSTEINER BIER
7278 Davos Monstein/GR
081 420 30 60
www.biervision-monstein.ch

INTERESTING SITES
- The Wiesen viaduct crossing on the Rhaetian Railway
- The waterfall at Sertig Sand
- The Walser houses in Monstein

FREIAMT

BETWEEN BÜNZ AND LINDENBERG

AG

STARTING POINT	DESTINATION
MURI AG	**WOHLEN**
BEER	DIFFICULTY
LONZI	**HIKE**
MAP	
SHEET 225	LENGTH OF THE HIKE
(ZURICH)	**5H, 19KM**
INTERESTING SIGHT	DIFFERENCE IN HEIGHT
THE WOHLEN STRAW MUSEUM	CLIMB 440 M DESCENT 470 M

NATURALLY CLOUDY BLONDE

 ORANGE-GOLD

 PEANUT

 MALTY

BITTERNESS

5
4
3
2
1

SWEETNESS

5
4
3
2
1

DESCRIPTION OF THE JOURNEY

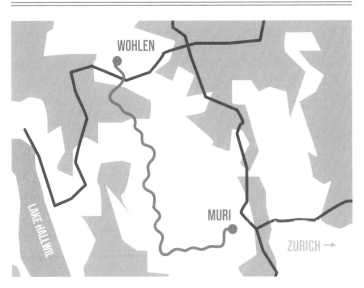

Muri (459 m) → Buttwill → Guggibad (722 m) → Brandholz → Unter Niesenberg → Büttikon → Wohlen AG (423 m)

The entire hike is well indicated. However, the path from Unter Niesenberg to Brandholz is only marked from the forest at the exit of the village. This hike is very diverse and entertaining, with little asphalt. You have a lovely view of the Alps at many points during the hike. From Muri train station it's a gentle climb to Buttwil village. The highest point of this hike is nearby the Gasthof Guggibad. Between Brandholz and Unter Niesenberg are two beautiful forest ponds.

These areas are equipped with benches, fire-pits and fountains. Shortly after Büttikon the path leads down to Wohlen.

Near the station, go through an underpass under the train tracks then continue straight on Bollmoosweg. Turn right onto Wehrlistrasse then left onto Friedhofstrasse and continue to the roundabout. At the roundabout turn slightly to the right onto Zentralstrasse, follow it until the next roundabout. Then, continue on Kappelstrasse. After just a few steps you'll reach the Chappelehof, where you can find seasonal beers from the Bünzwasser brewery. From here to train station takes about fifteen minutes. You can shorten this by taking the bus from Kirchplatz.

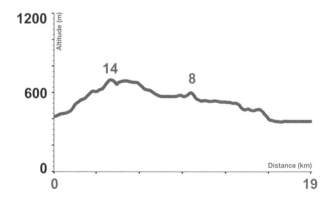

RETURN

Muri station is on the train line Lenzburg-Luzern.

BÜNZWASSER
Jurastrasse 8
Wohlen AG
www.buenzwasser.ch

KULTURBEIZ CHAPPELEHOF
Kapellstrasse 4
5610 Wohlen AG
056 621 33 20
www.chappelehof.ch

INTERESTING SIGHT
· The Wohlen Straw Museum

GEISSBERG

FROM THE WATER TOWER TO THE VALLEY OF METTAU

AG

STARTING POINT

TURGI

DESTINATION

HOTTWIL

BEER

FLÖSSERBRÄU

MAP

SHEET 215
(ZURICH)

SHEET 214
(LIESTAL)

INTERESTING SIGHT

THE RUINS OF
BESSERSTEIN CASTLE

DIFFICULTY

HIKE

LENGTH OF THE HIKE

5H, 18KM

DIFFERENCE IN HEIGHT

CLIMB 550 M
DESCENT 490 M

 **5.0%** ALCOHOL CONTENT

NON-FILTERED
NATURALLY
CLOUDY
TOP-FERMENTED

 NATURALLY CLOUDY

 SPICY

 REFRESHING

BITTERNESS	SWEETNESS
5	5
4	4
3	3
2	2
1	1

DESCRIPTION OF THE JOURNEY

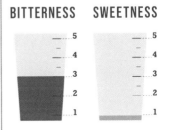

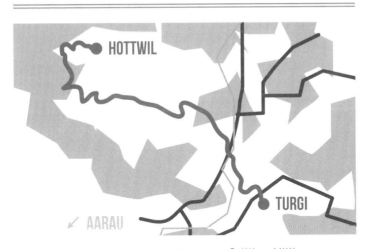

Turgi (342 m) → Ruine Freudenau → Stilli → Villigen
→ Besserstein → Geissberg Chameren (700 m)
→ Bürersteig → Laubberg → Hottwil (418 m)

Turgi is located on the train line between Baden and
Aarau.

From the station, follow the path that takes you to the ruins
of Freudenau. On the banks of the Limmat and the Aare,
you can see trees that have been gnawed on and felled by
beavers. A fire-pit has been installed at the ruins.

From the ruins, walk five minutes down the river to the Stilli bridge. Cross the bridge and follow the path in the direction of Geissberg, Bürersteig. This leads to the other side of the Aare and the villages of Stilli and Villigen.

Walk through the forest, climbing the eastern slope of the Geissberg. It's worth making a short detour to the ruins of Besserstein (with spots for a fire) for its amazing view.

Continuing along the path through the forest in the direction of Geissberg Chameren, you will pass by two mountain huts. Almost without realizing it, you will have made your way down a 150-meter change in altitude to reach Chameren, on the western slope of the Geissberg. This viewpoint is also equipped with a fire-pit.

Then, go down to Bürersteig (Laufenburg-Brugg Post bus), where you turn right to reach the Laubberg, the next viewpoint.

The descent of the Laubberg (signpost "Wil") takes you onto an arc that passes below the summit before heading south. After a curve, this arc heads north and passes below the summit of the Laubberg once again at a lower altitude. The path takes a sharp left above Hottwil.

Here, leave the track and follow the Helsana trail until you reach Hottwil. This path is straight for a short distance and then turns left. When you arrive at a grove of trees, the path turns left again. Just before you get to a farm, the path takes a right turn and leads straight to the village.

A road sign will point you in the direction of the Gasthaus Bären, where you can enjoy the local beer of Hottwil, the Flösserbräu.

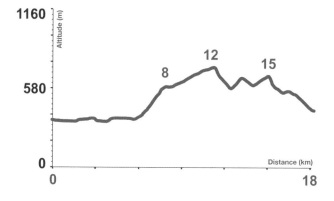

RETURN

As you leave the Gasthaus Bären turn right, and after about three minutes you reach the Hottwil Wendeplatz bus stop where you can catch a bus to Brugg and Laufenburg / Frick.

GASTHAUS BÄREN
Dorfstrasse 19
5277 Hottwil
062 875 11 45
www.baeren-hottwil.ch

FLÖSSERBIER
Hauptstrasse 80
5277 Hottwil
079 751 93 83
www.floesserbier.ch

INTERESTING SIGHTS
*   The water tower at the confluence of the Aare, Reuss and Limmat rivers
*   The ruins of Besserstein castle

GERSAUERSTOCK
OR VITZNAUERSTOCK

THE MOUNTAIN WITH TWO NAMES

LU

STARTING POINT

VITZNAU

DESTINATION

VITZNAU

BEER

URBRÄU

DIFFICULTY

ALPINE HIKE

MAP

SHEET 235

(ROTKREUZ)

LENGTH OF THE ALPINE HIKE

6H, 9KM

INTERESTING SIGHT

WISSIFLUHBAHN

DIFFERENCE IN HEIGHT

CLIMB AND DESCENT 1020 M

5.0% ALCOHOL CONTENT

BLONDE
FILTERED
AND BOTTOM-
FERMENTED

 DARK GOLD

 SPICY, FULL OF CHARACTER

 SLIGHTLY SPICY

BITTERNESS	SWEETNESS
5	5
4	4
3	3
2	2
1	1

DESCRIPTION OF THE JOURNEY

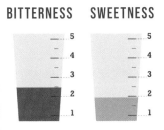

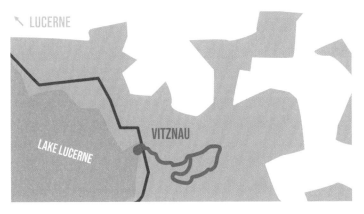

Vitznau Post (435 m) → Lower cable car station of Wissifluh 15 minutes
Lower cable car station of Wissifluh
→ Wissiflue 1½ hours or by the train
Wissiflue → Vitznauerstock (1451 m)
→ Fälmisegg 2¼ hours
Fälmisegg → Vitznau 1½ hours or Fälmisegg
→ Hinterbergen 30 minutes and return to Vitznau by train

The town of Vitznau is on the Brunnen-Küssnacht bus line at the foot of Mount Rigi. At the bus stop Vitznau station, take the Gufferiweg and the street Oberdorf to get to the lower cable car station of Wissifluh. The best way to find your bearings is to locate the cable cars, which are visible from afar. In less than 15 minutes, you will arrive at the lower cable car station of Wissifluh and Hinterberg.

For this hike, you must be surefooted and the trail must be dry. The trickiest passages are in the forest. For this reason, you must wait a few days after it has rained so that the trail isn't too slippery. As there are ladders along the trail, this hike is not suitable for dogs.

From the lower station climb through the forest until the upper cable car station of Wissifluh, or you can take the cable car.

You must make a reservation to take the cable car. From the upper station, go to the mountain inn Wissiflue, which has a panoramic terrace overlooking the lake. A scene from the police series Tatort was filmed here. Here, you can find products from local organic farms and fresh water from the local spring. The cable car is operated from the restaurant's kitchen.

At the restaurant, turn left onto the Gersauerstock or the Vitznauerstock. After a curvy path through a pasture, the trail leads into the forest. The trail is narrow and steep, and leads to the summit, where there is a view of the slopes.

Before beginning your descent toward Fälmisegg, make a detour to the panoramic viewpoint (5 minutes, trail indicated) where you can see the other side. Here you have a wider view than from the summit. Like the climb, the descent to Fälmisegg requires caution. You have to climb over a rocky outcrop with a ladder.

Option 1: From Fälmisegg, take the hiking trail in the direction of Vitznau via Saint Antoni. It follows a gorge and cuts through a forest with many visible blocks of stone, which are the remains of a rock fall. Then, make your way back to the trail leading to the lower cable car station of Wissifluh.

Option 2: From Fälmisegg, take the hiking trail in the direction of the cable car of Hinterbergen, which is used to return to Vitznau.

From the lower station, go to the bus stop Vitznau station. This is the same station where you arrived in Vitznau. Just next to this stop is a pier from where you can take a boat ride and make the most of the stations and bus stops around the lake.

On the boats that sail on the lake, you can drink the beer Urbräu, which is specially produced by the Ramseier brewery for the sailing company of Lake Lucerne.

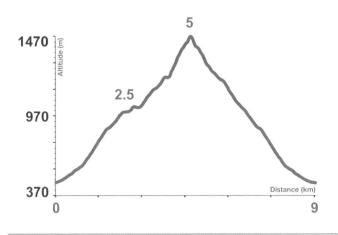

BERGGASTHAUS UND SEILBAHN WISSIFLUH
041 397 13 27
www.wissifluh.ch

RESTAURANT UND SEILBAHN HINTERBERGEN
041 397 16 87
www.hinterbergen.ch

URBRÄU
041 367 61 61
www.urbraeu.ch

SCHIFFFAHRTSGESELLSCHAFT VIERWALDSTÄTTERSEE
041 367 67 67
www.lakelucerne.ch

INTERESTING SIGHT
- The cable car of Wissifluh, over one hundred years old.

GOTTÉRON

ON THE ROSTIGRABEN

STARTING POINT	**DESTINATION**
# ST. ANTONI	# FRIBOURG
BEER	**DIFFICULTY**
## FRI-MOUSSE	## HIKE
MAP	
## SHEET 243 (BERNE)	**LENGTH OF THE HIKE**
## SHEET 242 (AVENCHES)	# 3H15, 11KM
INTERESTING SIGHT	**DIFFERENCE IN HEIGHT**
## THE OLD CITY OF # FRIBOURG	CLIMB 290 M DESCENT 380 M

4.8% ALCOHOL CONTENT

BLONDE
NON-FILTERED
NATURALLY
CLOUDY

 ORANGE

 FRUITY, BREAD

 MALTY, STRAW

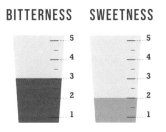

BITTERNESS   SWEETNESS

DESCRIPTION OF THE JOURNEY

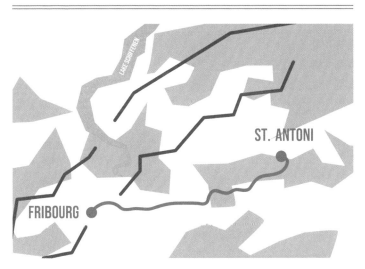

St. Antoni (715 m) → Weissenbach (647 m)
→ Pfaffenhölzli (781 m) → Juch → Ameismüli
→ Galterengraben or the gorges of Gottéron
→ Sarine (549 m) → Fribourg (629 m)

The bus stop St. Antoni Dorf is on the Fribourg
Schwarzenburg line.

From St. Antoni, follow the hiking trail in the

direction of Weissenbach. After a short climb, follow the path between the sandstone blocks in the Seligraben. In Weissenbach, two paths lead to Tafers (Tavel in French). Take the one going to Tafers Chrüz via the Pfaffenhözli. Walk up through the forest until you arrive on the side of the hill, from where there is a beautiful view of the Alps on the Fribourg side. Sometimes, some of the summits of the Bernese Oberland can be seen.

From the Pfafffenhölzi, follow the hiking trail in the direction of Ameismüli. After about 10 minutes, you will come to a nice picnic area with a place to make a fire and a lovely view. Then, continue via Juch until you reach the bus stop Tafers Chrüz. Cross the road and continue on to Ameismüli.

This is where the trail across the gorge begins. There are many signs warning about the dangers of slides, falling rocks or ice during specific weather conditions (storm, heavy rain, thawing) and stating that the trail is to be used at your own risk. The trail is closed if the weather conditions are particularly dangerous. If the trail is closed, you can return to Tafers Chrüz and take the bus, or take another trail that goes to Fribourg by passing to the north of the gorge.

The Gottéron River has carved a gorge into the sandstone. The trail, fitted with many stairs and wooden or metal footbridges, crosses through a beautiful virgin forest. The layers of sandstone are clearly visible. In some places, calcareous tufa has formed on the banks of the small tributaries. At one of the rest areas, you can even see the stalactites in a waterfall. The wooden footbridges and steps can be slippery when wet.

In the lower part of the gorge, the path follows a small road. The restaurant Pinte des trois canards is located in an old mill. The next step is the Buvette du Petit Train, with its garden and small model train. Passing through an old gate, you will come to the street Schmiedgasse, also called rue des Forgerons, where the Gottéron River disappears into the ground. Cross the Sarine River via the covered Bern Bridge. A map of the town is available on the bridge.

Continue straight on towards la place du Petit-St-Jean, from where the street rue de la Samaritaine begins. The restaurant l'Auberge du Soleil Blanc, at 29 rue de la Samaritaine, serves a local beer called Fri-Mousse. The brewery, at 19 rue de la Samaritaine, is open Saturdays from 8 am to 4 pm and the store Près de chez vous also sells this beer (20 m from the brewery).

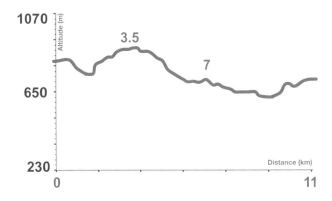

RETURN

From place du Petit-St-Jean, take either bus number 4 in the direction of Fribourg station or walk along the path St-Jacques. It will take about 35 minutes on foot, already counted in the duration of the hike. The marking isn't yellow, but blue with a yellow shell. You first go down the street rue de la Samaritaine and the street Stalden. Then take the street Grand Rue (The Swiss Museum of Sewing Machines and Unusual Objects is located at 58 Grand Rue), cross la Place de Notre Dame (Gutenberg Museum) and then the pedestrian quarter until you reach the station.

PINTE DES TROIS CANARDS
chemin du Gottéron 102
1700 Fribourg
026 321 28 22

BUVETTE DU PETIT TRAIN
chemin du Gottéron 17
1700 Fribourg
026 322 57 48
www.chemindeferdugotteron.ch

RESTAURANT SOLEIL BLANC
rue de la Samaritaine 29
1700 Fribourg
026 322 21 33

BRASSERIE ARTISANALE DE FRIBOURG
rue de la Samaritaine 19
1700 Fribourg
www.fri-mousse.ch

INTERESTING SIGHTS
- The Gorges of Gottéron
- The old town of Fribourg
- Swiss Museum of Sewing Machines and Unusual Objects Grand Rue 58
  www.museewassmer.com
- The Gutenberg Museum Place Notre Dame 16
  www.gutenbergmuseum.ch

GURTEN

ON THE BERNESE HAUSBERG

BE

STARTING POINT	**DESTINATION**
# KÖNIZ	# WABERN
BEER	**DIFFICULTY**
WABRÄU BLONDE	
MAP	**HIKE**
# SHEET 243	
	LENGTH OF THE HIKE
(BERN)	# 2H, 7KM
INTERESTING SIGHT	
	DIFFERENCE IN HEIGHT
AN OBSERVATION TOWER	CLIMB 310 M
	DESCENT 320 M

5.2% ALCOHOL CONTENT

BLONDE
NON-FILTERED
NATURALLY
CLOUDY

 GOLDEN YELLOW

 FRESH FRUITY

 SLIGHT HINT OF CITRUS FRUIT

BITTERNESS SWEETNESS

DESCRIPTION OF THE JOURNEY

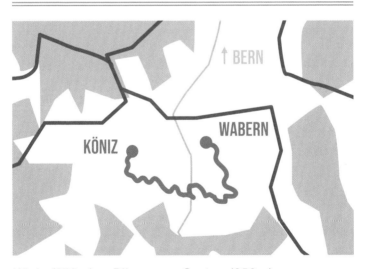

Köniz (572 m) → Blinzern → Gurten (858 m)
→ Wabern (560 m)

Köniz is on the train line between Bern and
Schwarzenburg.

"Wanderweg" is the only destination on the hiking
sign at Köniz station.

If you follow this direction, you will arrive in downtown Köniz. From there, follow the hiking path in the direction of Gurten Kulm. For the first fifteen minutes you will walk on the sidewalk of a very busy road. If you want to avoid this first stage, you can take bus number 16 from downtown Köniz to Köniz Blinzern. From Blinzern, you start walking on wide forest tracks with a gentle slope. You reach the western signal with very little effort, where you will find an observation tower, a play area and some restaurants. It is worth going up the tower to see the view of the Pilatus, the Bernese Oberland and the Fribourg Alps. You can also see a lot of the Jura Arc and, of course, the city of Bern. The descent to Wabern begins at the upper station of the Gurten funicular. First, climb a little way to get to the eastern signal, which is two meters higher than the western signal. The best path goes in an arc across the meadows and the forests, which leads down to the Gurten funicular lower station. Here you can see an old mash tun from the former Gurten brewery. The buildings are now occupied by various companies. Cross the entire zone until you reach a cliff overhanging the premises of the Wabräu brewery. At the entrance to the zone, there is an orientation panel to help you find the brewery (the opening times are available on the brewery's website).

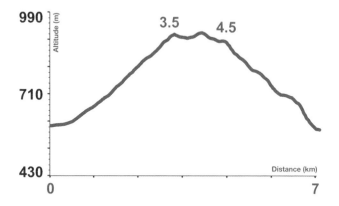

RETURN

Go back to the cable car at Gurten and then turn left to reach Wabern station in three minutes.

RESTAURANTS TAPIS ROUGE ET BEL ÉTAGE
Gurten
031 970 33 33
www.gurtenpark.ch

WABRÄU
Gurtenareal Dorfstrasse
3084 Wabern
031 961 89 51
www.wabraeu.ch

INTERESTING SIGHTS
· The observation tower
· The play area with the miniature train

HAGLERE

A MARSHY SITE WITH WONDERFUL VIEWPOINTS

LU

STARTING POINT	DESTINATION
FLÜELI HÜTTLENE	**SÖRENBERG**

BEER	DIFFICULTY
ENTLEBUCHER BIER	**ALPINE HIKE**

MAP

SHEET 244 (ESCHOLZMATT)

LENGTH OF THE ALPINE HIKE

5H15, 12KM

INTERESTING SIGHTS

MARSH ON LIST OF UNESCO WORLD HERITAGE SITES ENTLEBUCH BIOSPHERE

DIFFERENCE IN HEIGHT

CLIMB 1050 M
DESCENT 820 M

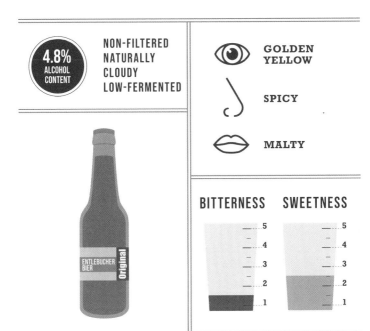

NON-FILTERED
NATURALLY
CLOUDY
LOW-FERMENTED

4.8% ALCOHOL CONTENT

ENTLEBUCHER BIER — Original

GOLDEN YELLOW

SPICY

MALTY

BITTERNESS

5
4
3
2
1

SWEETNESS

5
4
3
2
1

DESCRIPTION OF THE JOURNEY

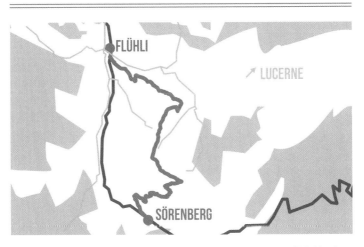

FLÜHLI

LUCERNE

SÖRENBERG

Flüeli Hüttlene (915 m) → Bleikechopf → Haglere (1949 m)
→ Teufimattsattel → Sörenberg (1166 m)

lüeli is on the Schüpfheim-Sörenberg post bus line.

From the Flüeli Hüttiene bus stop, follow the path until
you get to Bleikechopf. For a short time before
crossing the bridge, you will walk along the road. After
the bridge, turn left. For the first half hour, you walk
along a narrow paved street where cars are allowed.
This is the only downside to this hike. Shortly

afterwards, the path moves away from the narrow street and climbs up a steep, wooded slope. On this narrow path you need to be surefooted. Next, you go past an alpine pasture on the Bleuchekopf, the first peak of this hike. You will reach the second peak by crossing a marshy area with many pines, called the Haglere. Here, you have a beautiful view, especially of the Titlis region. Make your way down to Soerenberg via Teufimattsattel. You first make your way through a forest. Across the meadows you can catch sight of the majestic Schrattenfluh and the Brienzer Rothorn. Turn left on the main road in Soerenberg and a few meters further along you will reach the Bäckerstube restaurant where you can enjoy some Entlebucher beer. During my visit, the restaurant was unfortunately closed, but you can also find the local beer next door at the Volg store.

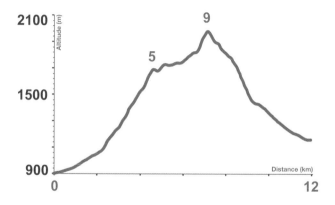

RETURN

Walk about 400 meters up the valley until you reach the post bus stop with connecting services to Schüpfheim train station.

RESTAURANT BÄCKERSTUBE
Rothornstrasse 19
6174 Sörenberg/LU
041 488 13 61
www.baeckerstube.ch

VOLG
Rothorn-Center 1
6174 Sörenberg/LU
041 488 11 33

ENTLEBUCHER BIER
Farb 3
6162 Entlebuch
041 480 01 64
www.entlebucher-bier.ch

INTERESTING SIGHTS
- The marsh which is a UNESCO world heritage site
- The Entlebuch biosphere

HEITERSBERG

A FOREST LAKE AND A WILD, ROCKY LANDSCAPE

AG

STARTING POINT	DESTINATION
REPPISCHHOF	**BADEN**

BEER	DIFFICULTY
MÜLLER BRÄU	**HIKE**

MAP
SHEET 215
(BADEN)

SHEET 225
(ZURICH)

LENGTH OF THE HIKE

4H45, 18KM

INTERESTING SIGHT

THE CLIFF OF TÜFELS-CHÄLLER

DIFFERENCE IN HEIGHT

CLIMB 430 M
DESCENT 470 M

5.0% ALCOHOL CONTENT

BLONDE
NON-FILTERED
AND BOTTOM-
FERMENTED

 BLONDE

 FRUITY

 SLIGHT TASTE OF CEREAL

BITTERNESS	SWEETNESS

DESCRIPTION OF THE JOURNEY

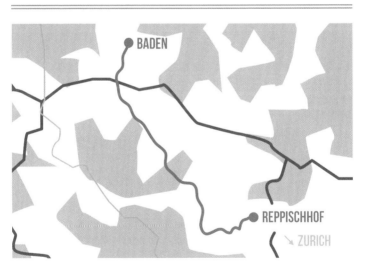

BADEN

REPPISCHHOF

ZURICH

Reppischhof (428 m) → Hasenberg → Heitersberg (735 m)
or Egelsee → Tüfels-Chäller → Baden (385 m)

Reppischhof is on the Dietikon-Bremgarten-Wohlen
rail line.

From the underground passage at the station, take the
exit to the left, then walk up hill passing the Gwinden
and Herrenberg restaurants, until the Hasenberg

restaurant. This climb has lovely landscapes, but you have to walk on asphalt most of the time.

There aren't many hiking signposts on the route, so you will need to have a look at the map from time to time in order to find the Hasenberg without any difficulty.

From the Hasenberg, take the path in the direction of Baden. The ground is now more natural and the path is well marked. Shortly after Hasenberg, you will have to choose between taking the hike going by the ridge of Heitersberg and going along Lake Egelsee. Both itineraries are wonderful. Both routes are about the same length and meet up at pt. 708. Then, continue along the trail weaving in and out of the forest with occasional views of the Limmat Valley or the Reuss Valley.

Just before Baden, you go through the forest of Tüfels-Chäller. After the last ice age, there was a huge landslide and it formed a wild landscape with rock formations, crevices and holes. The forest isn't maintained and becomes wilder the further in you go. By taking a path that is well laid out, you arrive at the edge of the forest and the old town of Baden. The path leads you through the town's gate. Then, continue straight on and cross the street Bahnhofstrasse to arrive at the station.

The beer made by the Müller brewery is served in many restaurants in Baden. In the summer, it's best to drink it on the brewery's terrace. To get there, take the underground passage below the platforms until you you arrive in front of the Coop supermarket. From there, take a left and climb the stairs. When you've reached the top of the stairs, take an immediate right. Cross a passage to get to the Dynamostrasse. To the right, you can already see the trees of the brewery. A few steps further and you arrive in front of the long tables under the old trees. When it's nice, the terrace is open every day in the summer.

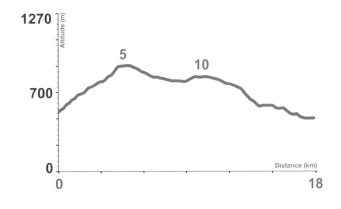

GASTHOF HERRENBERG
044 740 82 56
www.gasthof-herrenberg.ch

HOTEL RESTAURANT RYOKAN, HASENBERG
056 648 40 00
www.hotel-hasenberg.ch

BIERGARTEN BADEN
Dynamostrasse
5400 Baden
079 598 50 32
www.biergartenbaden.ch

BRAUEREI MÜLLER
Dynamostrasse 8
5400 Baden
056 203 06 06
www.brauerei-mueller.ch

INTERESTING SIGHTS
· Lake Egelsee
· Tüfels-Chäller, the rocky landscape

HOCHASTLER

BEAUTIFUL VIEW OF THE RHONE VALLEY

VS

STARTING POINT	DESTINATION
RARON	**BÜRCHEN HASEL**
BEER	DIFFICULTY
BÜRCHNER BIER	
MAP	**ALPINE HIKE**
SHEET 274	
(VISP)	LENGTH OF THE ALPINE HIKE
	3H, 5KM
INTERESTING SIGHT	
VIEW POINT FROM THE HOCHASTLER	DIFFERENCE IN HEIGHT
	CLIMB 760 M DESCENT 60 M

4.8%
ALCOHOL
CONTENT

BLONDE
NON-FILTERED
NATURALLY
CLOUDY

 GOLDEN
YELLOW

 MODERATELY
SPICY

 MALTY

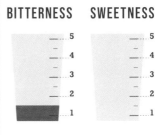

BITTERNESS   SWEETNESS

DESCRIPTION OF THE JOURNEY

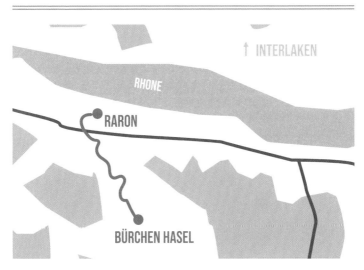

Raron (620 m) → Birch → Hochastler
→ Bürchen Hasel (1340 m)

Raron is on the railroad line between Lausanne
and Brig.

The entire trail is marked as a hiking trail (yellow), but
the bottom third of the trail is more like an alpine
hike. All of the paths mentioned are indicated on the

FSTP map (2008 edition), but they weren't all marked when I took this hike in 2011.

From the station in Raron, go to the lower cable car station in the direction of Unterbaech (five minutes when following the white signs in the underground passage). At the lower cable car station of Raron-Unterbäch, take the trail leading to Bürchen (marker on the guardrail of the bridge). Zigzag up through the forest, which is scattered with pine and birch trees, in the direction of Birch.

You will come to a paved path. From Birch, the path is no longer marked. With the help of the map, there's no problem finding the trail. A small street and a trail both lead to Bürchen. The trail cuts across this small street no less than five times before it runs into a narrow street at the foot of Hochastler. Follow this narrow street for about 200 meters and then take the path to the left in the direction of Hochastler (signpost). Very shortly after, you will see two more signposts indicating Hochastler.

After that, the trail is no longer marked but it isn't a problem. The Hochastler panoramic look-out can be seen from far away thanks to its radio tower and big cross.

The wonderful view during the climb is well worth the effort. Beyond the Rhone Valley you can see the Lötschental mountains and even further the ramp of the Lötschental. To the south-west you can see Unterbäch, the Rütli (mountain meadow) of Swiss women (see the film *Verliebte Feinde*).

From Hochastler, follow the same path back to the last marker. From there, go straight on in the direction of Bürchen, once again on an unmarked trail. Once you've arrived at the Obscha post bus stop (indicated on the map, but without the name), you're back on the route. From there, follow the marked path in the direction of Hasel. It first follows the road and then climbs a steep slope and passes the church, after which it meets back up with the road. Here, turn right at the town store, where you can buy the beer Bürchner.

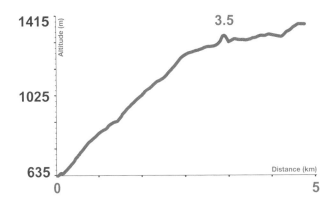

RETURN

The town store is located directly next to the post office of Hasel in Bürchen, where the post bus to Visp leaves from.

VOLG
Bürchen Hasel
027 934 27 72

BÜRCHNER BIER
078 778 24 19

INTERESTING SIGHTS
- The panoramic view from Hochastler
- Unterbäch, the Rütli (mountain meadow) of Swiss women

HOMBERG

ON A RANGE OF HILLS ABOVE THE AARGOVIAN SEETAL

AG

STARTING POINT	DESTINATION
SEON	**BEINWIL AM SEE**
BEER	DIFFICULTY
MÜLLER BRÄU	**HIKE**
MAP	
SHEET 224 (OLTEN)	
SHEET 225 (ZURICH)	LENGTH OF THE HIKE
	4H, 14KM
INTERESTING SIGHT	
	DIFFERENCE IN HEIGHT
LAKE HALLWIL	CLIMB 540 M DESCENT 460 M

5.0% ALCOHOL CONTENT

BLONDE NON-FILTERED AND BOTTOM-FERMENTED

 LIGHT

 FRUITY

 WHEATY

BITTERNESS SWEETNESS

DESCRIPTION OF THE JOURNEY

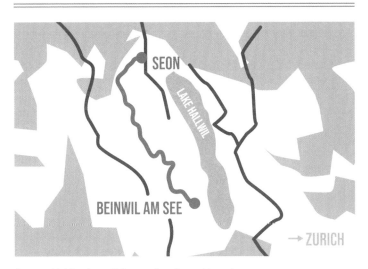

Seon (446 m) → Dürrenäsch → Homberg
→ Hochwacht (788 m) → Beinwil am See (519 m)

The town of Seon is on the railroad line in the Valley of See (Seetalbahn) between Lenzburg and Lucerne.

From the station in Seon, follow the track that goes by the Sibe Zwingstei and Dürrenäsch on the Homberg. On many occasions you have an unrestricted view of the Alps, the Jura, the Black Forest and the Plateau. In the mountain restaurant Homberg in Ober Flügelberg, you can enjoy a pint of Müller Bräu. From the mountain restaurant, walk 10 more minutes to get to the Hochwacht Lookout Tower, offering a beautiful panoramic view stretching from Mount Säntis to the Bernese Oberland. From Hochwacht, it is a 35 minute walk down to the station Beinwil am See, which is also on the Seetalbahn railroad line.

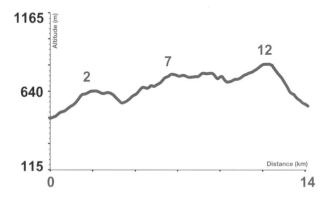

BERGRESTAURANT HOMBERG
062 771 10 53
www.homberg-reinach.ch

BRAUEREI MÜLLER
Dynamostrasse 8
5400 Baden
056 203 0606
www.brauerei-mueller.ch

INTERESTING SIGHT
· Lake Hallwil

HONASP

OLD AND NEW TRACK LINKING ZURICH TO WINTERTHUR

ZH

STARTING POINT	**DESTINATION**
# KEMPTTHAL	# NÜRENSDORF
BEER	**DIFFICULTY**
## SCHLOSSQUELL	
MAP	## WALK
# SHEET 216	**LENGTH OF THE HIKE**
## (FRAUENFELD)	# 1H30, 5KM
INTERESTING SIGHT	**DIFFERENCE IN HEIGHT**
## OLD FACTORY BUILDING	CLIMB 140 M DESCENT 100 M

5.2% ALCOHOL CONTENT

BROWN
NON-FILTERED
NATURALLY
CLOUDY

 DARK BLONDE

 SLIGHTLY MALTY

 CARAMEL

BITTERNESS   SWEETNESS

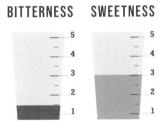

DESCRIPTION OF THE JOURNEY

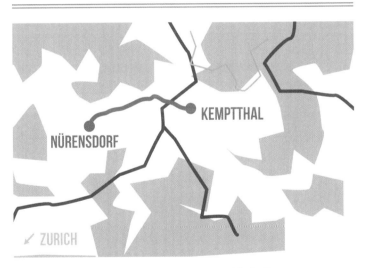

Kemptthal (469 m) → Winterberg → Kleinikon
→ Honasp → Hakab → Nürensdorf (505 m)

Kemptthal is on the railroad line Zurich-Winterthur.
The small station next to the old Maggi factory sits in
a narrow valley passed through by all railroad and
road traffic between Zurich and Winterthur.
Follow the hiking trail in the direction of Nürensdorf.
This path begins with a climb, shortly after which the

path levels out and highway noise mostly disappears.
Go through the towns of Winterberg and Kleinikon.
Next, go in the direction of Hakab and cross a plateau
with large fields, meadows and the forest of Honasp.
There is very often a magnificent view of the Alps.
From Hakab, walk along the banks of a small stream,
which descends to Nürensdorf, until the intersection
next to the restaurant Bären. At the time of carts and
horse-drawn carriages, this was the main route
between Winterthur and Zurich.

From this intersection, take a right and walk by the
library. When the Schlossbraui brewery is open, there
is a sign on the sidewalk. A little further, you get to
the brewery where you can drink the beer
Schlossquell on Saturday from 10 am to noon (in
winter, the brewery is also open Friday evening).
Those who don't make the opening hours can buy this
beer in the store Volg which is in front of the
restaurant Bären.

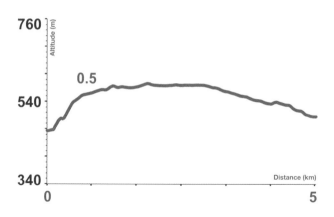

RETURN

Go back to the intersection of the Bären restaurant. There are three bus stops here (Post Lindauerstrasse and Sennhütte), which have direct links to the stations in Winterthur, Effretikon, and Bassersdorf.

SCHLOSSBRAUI NÜRENSDORF
Brauereiweg 3
Postfach 223
8309 Nürensdorf
www.schlossquell.ch

VOLG
Lindauerstrasse 2
8309 Nürensdorf
044 836 52 16

RESTAURANT BÄREN
Alte Winterthurerstrasse 45
8309 Nürensdorf
044 836 49 00
www.baeren-nuerensdorf.ch

INTERESTING SIGHT
- The old factory building near the station in Kemptthal

HÖNGGERBERG

THREE VERY DIFFERENT DISTRICTS OF ZURICH

ZH

STARTING POINT

ZURICH AFFOLTERN

BEER

STEINFELS

MAP

MAP OF THE CITY

ZURICH

INTERESTING SIGHT

THE BERNOUILLI HOUSES

DESTINATION

ZURICH KREIS 5

DIFFICULTY

WALK

LENGTH OF THE HIKE

1H30, 6KM

DIFFERENCE IN HEIGHT

CLIMB 100 M

DESCENT 150 M

5.3% ALCOHOL CONTENT

BLONDE
NON-FILTERED
NATURALLY
CLOUDY

 GOLDEN YELLOW

 FRUITY

 FRUITY WITH A TASTE OF BANANA

BITTERNESS **SWEETNESS**

DESCRIPTION OF THE JOURNEY

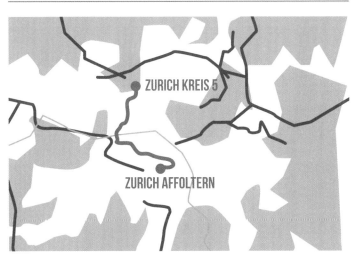

Zurich Affoltern (456 m) → Hönggerberg → Limmat → Zurich Kreis 5 (400 m)

You can get to the Rehnhausplatz of Zurich Affoltern by taking bus 37 from Affoltern or by taking bus 62 from Oerlikon. There are bus stops on each side of the intersection.
When you get off in front of the restaurant Löwen, take the underground passage below the

Wehntalerstrasse to get to the bus stop across the street. Doing so will put you on the hiking trail in the direction of Zurich Höngg. It first climbs into the forest and later goes along a ravine. At the point where three paths meet, one of which descends to a bridge, the marker is not easily seen.

A half-erased arrow on a 50 cm stone will point you in the right direction. After passing a fire-pit, you will reach the edge of the forest and then a sports field. Just after that, there is a beautiful view of the Limmat Valley and of Zurich, and you can even see the Alps when the sky is clear.

Continue on this hiking trail and go down to Höngg until the Regensdorferstrasse. Now, leave the path and take the Wieslergasse, which descends until the Imbisbühlstrasse. Then cross the Limmattalstrasse and continue following it on the left until you arrive at the Hohenklingenstrasse. From there, follow the footpath in the direction of Albisrieden. This will follow the same route as Hohenklingenstrasse until you reach the street Am Wettingertobel. Walk down this street.

You will quickly come to a footpath leading you to Vorhaldenstrasse. Cross the Winzerstrasse and then take the path Winzerhalde, which is a little to the right. This will take you to the hydroelectric plant in Höngg.

From the plant, take a left and climb the Limmat (street signpost "Im Giessen") until Hardeggsteg. Cross the Limmat and walk by the Bernouilli houses until you reach Hardturmwegsteg, where you take a right on the bank of the Limmat (in the same direction as the current). This way, you avoid a part of the road. Continue along the river until Dammsteg, just before the next railroad viaduct, and cross the Limmat once again. Next, go straight ahead and walk past the old Löwenbräu brewery to arrive at the Limmatstrasse. Cross it and take a right to get to the Roggenstrasse. Take Roggenstrasse until you find Heinrichstrasse, then turn right at number 267.

At this address you can drink locally brewed Steinfels beer in the brasserie-restaurant of the same name.

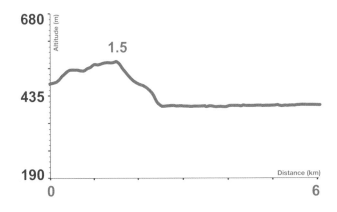

RETURN

When the Heinrichstrasse runs into the street Hardstrasse, the Escher-Wyss-Platz is about 200 meters to the right. Several trams and buses stop here. Or, you can continue for about 600 more meters to get to the station S-Bahn (suburban trains) Hardbrücke.

RESTAURANT STEINFELS
Heinrichstrasse 267
8005 Zurich
044 271 10 30
www.steinfels-zuerich.ch

INTERESTING SIGHTS
· The Bernouilli houses
· The hydroelectric plant in Höngg
  To visit, call 058 319 49 60

HUTTWIL

THE "GRENZPFAD NAPFBERGLAND" BORDER PATH

BE

STARTING POINT	DESTINATION
ST.URBAN	**HUTTWIL**

BEER	DIFFICULTY
NAPFGOLD	**HIKE**

MAP	
SHEET 224 (OLTEN)	
SHEET 234 (WILLISAU)	LENGTH OF THE HIKE
	5H, 20KM

INTERESTING SIGHT	
THE WET GRASSLANDS OF **THE ROTTAL**	DIFFERENCE IN HEIGHT
	CLIMB 520 M DESCENT 340 M

5.8% ALCOHOL CONTENT

BLONDE NON-FILTERED AND BOTTOM-FERMENTED

 BLONDE

 NUTTY

 MALTY

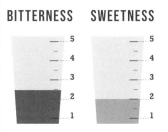

BITTERNESS

SWEETNESS

DESCRIPTION OF THE JOURNEY

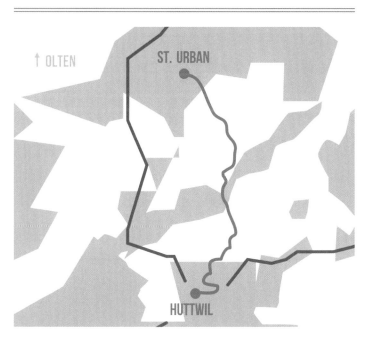

St. Urban (450 m) → Steihubel → Huttwilberg
→ Huttwil (638 m)

St. Urban is accessible via the train from Langenthal.
This hike is part of the Grenzpfad Napfbergland,

border path which runs in several stages from Langenthal to the Brienzer Rothorn. The entire trail is marked as a regional route with the number 65 on a green background on the yellow hiking signs. The entire trail is well marked.

In the former St. Urban monastery, there is a bakery and a butcher's shop where you can buy locally produced supplies for the hike (including cheese). The trail takes you across the wet grasslands of the Rottal. These are a natural attraction of national significance. This traditional way of farming is explained on signs. I suggest leaving route 65 to make a little detour in three different places.

Option 1: Instead of taking the route that leads to the St. Urban monastery, go under a large arch and enter the park. Walk through this magnificent park and return to the hiking trail, which is on the other side of the park (not marked).

Option 2: When you get to Steihubel, trail 65 goes down diagonally towards the road and follows it for about a kilometer. When you leave Steihubel, continue up the hill and then go straight down to the next intersection that leads back to the road.

Option 3: From the southern ridge of the Huttwilberg plateau, trail 65 goes straight down to the railroad station. It is worth making a little detour here and continuing eastwards along the ridge for about 600 meters. Then you will reach a lookout with a fabulous panoramic view. From there, take a right on the road that goes down towards the old town of Huttwil and and make your way to the railroad station via the Marktgasse.

You can enjoy enjoy Napfgold beer in several restaurants in Huttwil. You can find the list of these restaurants on the brewery's website.

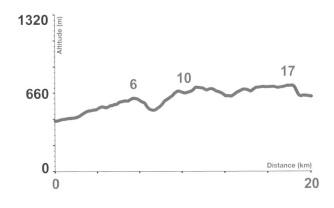

RETURN

Huttwil is on the Langenthal-Wolhusen railroad line.

BRAUEREI NAPF
Dorf 74 J
4942 Walterswil/BE
062 964 02 70
www.brauerei-napf.ch

INTERESTING SIGHTS
- St. Urban park
- The wet grasslands of the Rottal

KRAUCHTHAL

A SANDY BEACH, DUNES AND OLD QUARRIES

BE

STARTING POINT	DESTINATION
BURGDORF STEINHOF	# KRAUCHTHAL
BEER	DIFFICULTY
HÜBELERBIER	**HIKE**
MAP	
SHEET 233	LENGTH OF THE HIKE
(SOLOTHURN) AND THE BROCHURE ABOUT THE SANDSTONE QUARRY EDUCATIONAL TRAIL	**3H, 9KM**
INTERESTING SIGHT	DIFFERENCE IN HEIGHT
SANDSTEINLEHRPFAD SANDSTONE QUARRY EDUCATIONAL TRAIL	CLIMB 230 M DESCENT 200 M

5.0% ALCOHOL CONTENT

NON-FILTERED NATURALLY CLOUDY AND BOTTOM-FERMENTED

 AMBER

 SWEET AROMATIC

 FRUITY

BITTERNESS	SWEETNESS
5	5
4	4
3	3
2	2
1	1

DESCRIPTION OF THE JOURNEY

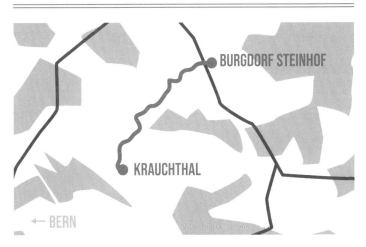

Burgdorf Steinhof (544 m) → Unterbärgetal
→ Krauchthal (585 m) → Sandstone quarry educational
trail on the Chrouchtubergg (707 m)

You can get to Burgdorf Steinhof using lines S4 and
S44 of the Bern S-Bahn. Some trains between Burgdorf
and Burgdorf Steinhof leave from platform 11, next to
platform 1.

Follow the hiking trail that crosses the Unterbärgetal in
the direction of the Krauchtal, which you will reach

after about two hours. The educational trail, the Sandsteinlehrpfad, begins on the main street in the village. It is marked with brown signs and takes you through the Chrouchtuberg (you need to be surefooted to make the detour via the Chrüzflue). Not only will you learn a lot about geology, but you will also be able to enjoy many of beautiful views as you walk. It takes one hour to complete the entire loop. The explanatory brochure about the educational trail costs 5 CHF and can be purchased at the local city office in Krauchthal, tel: 034 411 80 80.

You can buy the beer Krauchthal Hardeggerperle at the store Volg, which is near the post office on the road to Bollinger. Alternatively, you can try it at the Restaurant Hirschen, which you'll find on the road to Burgdorf.

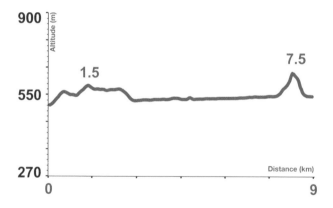

RETURN

Krauchtal is on the Hindelbank–Bolligen post bus line and these two towns are part of the Bern S-Bahn (suburban trains) network.

VOLG KRAUCHTHAL
Länggasse 17
3326 Krauchthal
034 411 14 64

BRAUEREI HARDEGGERPERLE
Hardegg 5
3326 Krauchthal-Hub
034 411 00 50
www.hardeggerperle.ch

RESTAURANT HIRSCHEN
Oberburgstrasse 11
3326 Krauchthal
034 411 14 31
www.hirschen-krauchthal.ch

INTERESTING SIGHT
· Sandstone quarry educational trail

INTERESTING FACTS!

NUMBERS

25%

25% OF BEER IS SOLD BOTTLED
AND ABOUT 32% IS CANNED.

483

TODAY, SWITZERLAND HAS MORE THAN 480
REGISTERED BREWERIES (483 IN SEPTEMBER
2014), WHICH PLACES IT IN THE TOP 10
WORLDWIDE IN PROPORTION TO THE NUMBER OF
INHABITANTS.

63 621

SWISS BEER (63,621 HL) IS
EXPORTED TO 34 COUNTRIES.
BEER IS IMPORTED (1,225,252 HL)
FROM 88 COUNTRIES.

1996

THE BREWERY WÄDI BRÄU WAS A PIONEER IN HEMP BEER AND WAS THE FIRST BREWERY IN THE WORLD TO BOTTLE HEMP BEER (1996).

3 431 928

IN TOTAL, BREWERIES PRODUCED 3,431,928 HECTOLITERS (3.43 MM HL) OF BEER IN 2014.

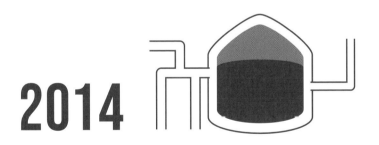

2014

THE AVERAGE CONSUMPTION OF BEER IN SWITZERLAND PER INHABITANT WAS 55.8 LITERS IN 2014.

LANGUAGES

(GERMAN)

"GUTEN TAG, EIN BIER BITTE"

(FRENCH)

"BONJOUR, UNE BIÈRE, S'IL VOUS PLAÎT"

(ENGLISH)

"HELLO, CAN I HAVE A BEER PLEASE ?"

(ITALIAN)

"BUONGIORNO, UNA BIRRA PER FAVORE"

(ROMANSH)

"ALLEGRA, INA BIERA PER PLASCHAIR"

BERE ØL OLUT
BIER
BEER BIRRA
BIER
CERVEJA ØL
PIWO
ÖL BIÈRE SÖR
PIVO MPIRA
CERVEZA

THE JOURNEY CONTINUES...

LAKE ARNI

A SMALL LAKE AT THE HEIGHT OF THE REUSS VALLEY

UR

STARTING POINT	DESTINATION
SILENEN DÄGERLOHN	# LAKE ARNI
BEER	DIFFICULTY
STIÄR BIÄR	**ALPINE HIKE**
MAP **SHEET 246** (KLAUSEN PASS)	
SHEET 256 (DISENTIS/MUSTÉR)	LENGTH OF THE ALPINE HIKE **3H15, 5KM**
INTERESTING SIGHT	DIFFERENCE IN HEIGHT
# LAKE ARNI	CLIMB 920 M DESCENT 60 M

5% ALCOHOL CONTENT

BLONDE
NON-FILTERED
NATURALLY
CLOUDY

GOLDEN BLONDE

TANGY, PEANUT

TANGY-BITTER

BITTERNESS

— 5
— 4
— 3
— 2
— 1

SWEETNESS

— 5
— 4
— 3
— 2
— 1

DESCRIPTION OF THE JOURNEY

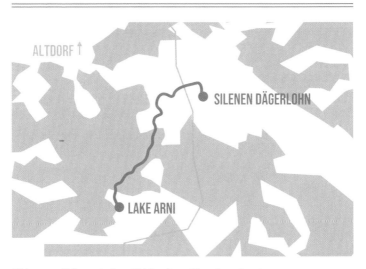

ALTDORF ↑

SILENEN DÄGERLOHN

LAKE ARNI

Silenen Dägerlohn (510 m) → Vorder Arni
→ Lake Arni (1370 m)

At the Dägerlohn bus stop, follow the hiking trail to
Lake Arni. Silenen Dägerlohn is on the Erstfeld–
Göschenen bus line.
This hike is ideal on a hot summer's day. If you leave
early enough, you can do most of the climb in the
shade. During a storm or after a lot of rain, the hike is

not recommended; you must cross a stream three times, which can become dangerous after a lot of rain.

After five minutes, turn left and follow the path in the direction of Reussdammwege. Cross the Reuss River and the highway, then bear right in the direction of Lake Arni. The trail is very well laid out and leads steadily up through the steep forest. Not many people pass through the lower part of the forest, so it is almost entirely covered with vegetation. Another trail emerges at pt. 676 (only on the map 1 / 25,000). From there, the path is easily seen until Lake Arni. It zigzags uphill to an altitude of 1300 meters. Then, you leave the forest and continue along meadow paths, from where there is a magnificent view. Shortly before you reach Lake Arni, you will cross the Arnisse Inn where you can have the local beer Stiär Biär.

It only takes ten minutes to go from this inn to the cable car station. But the path along the lake is so beautiful that it's worth taking your time. The top station is next to the Alpenblick inn.

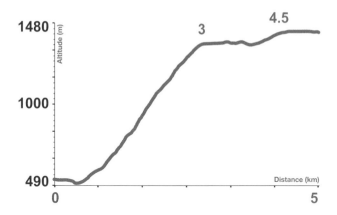

RETURN

With the cable car for Intschi. The restaurant Schäfli is located at the station for departure in the valley. The bus Erstfeld–Göschenen also stops there.

BERGGASTHAUS ARNISEE
041 883 12 83

KLEIN BRAUEREI
Stiär Biär AG
Postfach 48
6467 Schattdorf
041 870 65 80
www.kleinbrauerei.ch

CABLE CAR INTSCHI-ARNISEE
Gotthardstrasse
6476 Intschi
041 883 16 88
www.arnisee.ch

MOUNTAIN INN ALPENBLICK
041 883 03 42

GASTHAUS SCHÄFLI
Gotthardstrasse
6476 Intschi
041 883 11 40
www.schaefli-intschi.ch

INTERESTING SIGHT
• Lake Arni

LAKE TSEUZIER

FROM BISSE D'AYENT TO BISSE DU RO

VS

STARTING POINT	**DESTINATION**
# PRALAN	MONTANA LAKE YCOOR
BEER	**DIFFICULTY**
LA MARMOTTE BLANCHE	
MAP	**ALPINE HIKE**
# SHEET 273	
(MONTANA)	**LENGTH OF THE ALPINE HIKE**
	# 5H30, 20KM
INTERESTING SIGHTS	**DIFFERENCE IN HEIGHT**
BISSE D'AYENT (AYENT MOUNTAIN CANAL) BISSE DU RO (RO MOUNTAIN CANAL) LAKE TSEUZIER	CLIMB 600 M DESCENT 520 M

5.4% ALCOHOL CONTENT   WHEAT

DARK

CITRUS

MALTY

BITTERNESS   SWEETNESS

La Marmotte
la bière brassée à
CRANS-MONTANA

DESCRIPTION OF THE JOURNEY

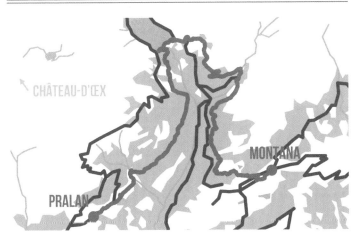

CHÂTEAU-D'ŒX

MONTANA

PRALAN

Pralan (1430m) → Bisse d'Ayent → Lake Tseuzier (1778m) → Bisse du Ro → Lake Grenon → Montana Lake Ycoor (1500m)

Pralan is on the bus line Sion–Anzère.

You must be surefooted and not be afraid of heights. The trails are very good but narrow and go along very steep slopes for long distances. Some sections are made up of wooden planks fastened to vertical rock faces.

You need to contort yourself a little or lower your head in certain spots. The most dangerous areas are secured by ropes or handrails. You will also need a flashlight to go through a small tunnel. The paths are always easily seen, but not often marked. The up-keep of the paths is carried out after all the snow has melted and the trail is normally open starting in mid-June.

From Pralan, follow the marked path towards La Fornirî. From there, the path goes along the bisse d'Ayent (the mountain canal of Ayent). In the lower part, follow the water. The canal is dry starting at the power plant in Chamarin, but mostly easy to see. When the intersections are no longer marked, stay near the canal. This very diversified trail sometimes looks like a walk, but proves to be more difficult in certain places. Flat in the beginning, it is steeper near the valley.

You walk most often in the forest, where countless laburnums flower in June. From the dam, you are rewarded with a breathtaking view. You can spend the night at the Barrage du Rawil restaurant.

Cross the dam towards the bisse du Ro (Ro mountain canal). After a short climb, the path descends towards the canal via the meadows and pasture of Er de Chermignon. The canal was built in the 14th century. Today, the hiking trail follows the path where water flowed long ago. From this open-air path, there is a panoramic view of the summits to the south, of the forest and the Ayent canal to the west, and of Lake Lienne below. Be prepared to catch a quick shower from a gushing waterfall.

From the end of the Ro canal, follow the marked path towards Lake Ycoor. The path winds through the forest and passes several houses before coming into a street that leads to the bus stop Pavillon du lac Grenon. The «Hôtel du Lac» is opposite the bus stop. Cross the street and take a right to walk along the lakeside to the hotel. The La Marmotte brewery is just next to it.

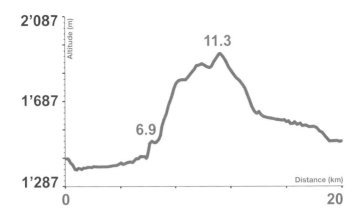

SHORTCUT

In the summer, a post bus can take you from Sion to the Dam of Rawil (with connections in Le Creux). It runs every day from mid-June to mid-August and every weekend from mid-August to mid-September. If you go down to the stop Le Samarin-Ehely, the hike takes 4 hours and 45 minutes, and only 3 and a half hours from the Dam of Rawil.

RETURN

Walk around Lake Grenon and take a right to go down to the bus stop Forum d'Ycoor (10 minutes), going by Lake Ycoor. Next, take the bus to Montana Station and go back down towards Sierre via the cable car. From the station in the valley, it only takes 5 minutes to get to the station of Sierre.

BRASSERIE LA MARMOTTE
Lac Grenon
3963 Crans-Montana
027 481 34 14
www.brasserie-la-marmotte.ch

RESTAURANT DU LAC DU BARRAGE DE TSEUZIER
Barrage du Rawyl
1972 Anzère
027 398 26 97

LAKE WOHLEN

RESERVOIR AND NATURAL PARADISE

BE

STARTING POINT	**DESTINATION**
# OBEREI	# BERN FELSENAU
BEER	**DIFFICULTY**
## BÄRNER MÜNTSCHI	
MAP	## HIKE
# SHEET 243	
# (BERN)	**LENGTH OF THE HIKE**
	# 4H30,17KM
INTERESTING SIGHT	
## NATURE RESERVE OF ## TEUFTALBUCHT	**DIFFERENCE IN HEIGHT**
	CLIMB 300 M DESCENT 380 M

4.8% ALCOHOL CONTENT

BROWN
NATURALLY
CLOUDY
AND BOTTOM-
FERMENTED

 BLACK

 ROASTED AROMA

 LIGHT

BITTERNESS   SWEETNESS

DESCRIPTION OF THE JOURNEY

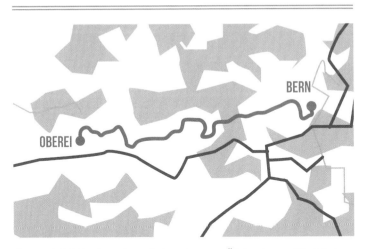

Oberei (595 m) → Jaggisbachau → Äbische → Wohlei
→ Wohleibrügg → Kappelenring → Neubrügg
→ Felsenau (534 m)

Oberei is on the post bus line between Bern and
Mühleberg.

The hiking sign at the bus stop has no name written
on it. Follow the path in the direction of Eiau (white
signs for cars). It will lead you down to the steep
southern bank of Lake Wohlen. Pass by some

sandstone cliffs via narrow trails and steep stairs. Continue on through some trees felled by beavers and you will arrive in the nature reserve of Teuftalbucht and the natural forest of Äbische.

Once at Äbische, you will come to an imposing farm with Highland cows. Since the herd contains a bull, crossing the pasture is at your own risk.

After a passage in a small forest, follow the reed-planted bank until Wohlei. Cross the lake via the bridge and go in the direction of Wohlen.

Looking down from the bridge, you will see an island with many waterfowls. Once you've arrived at the northern shore of Lake Wohlen, go under the Wohleibrügg and then continue the hike along the bank. Walk in the direction of the chapel bridge Kappelenbrügg / Kappelenbrücke and then in the direction of Neubrügg. Neubrügg is an old covered wooden bridge. Pass under it and continue to follow the bank of the Aare until Seftausteg, which takes about 15 minutes. The Seftausteg is a footbridge that is next to an old hydroelectric power plant. Cross the river via the Seftausteg and head upriver to get to the Felsenau brewery. You can buy the beer there during their 'ramp sale' hours, usually once a week. Many restaurants and bars in and around Bern serve Felsenau beer. You can find the full list on the brewery's website. The original destination for this hike was actually the Restaurant Felsenau, which was right near the brewery. Sadly, it burnt down in 2014 and has remained closed ever since.

RETURN

Just in front of the former restaurant is the bus stop Felsenau, where you can take bus number 21 to get to the central station of Bern.

BRAUEREI FELSENAU
Strandweg 34
3004 Bern
031 301 22 08
www.felsenau.ch

INTERESTING SIGHTS
- Nature reserve of Teuftalbucht
- Primary forest of Äbische

LOORENCHOPF

ZH

STARTING POINT	DESTINATION
MAUR	**ZURICH** SCHWAMENDINGEN
BEER	DIFFICULTY
PAUL 01	**HIKE**
MAP	
SHEET 226 (RAPPERSWIL)	
SHEET 225 (ZURICH)	LENGTH OF THE HIKE
	4H15, 17KM
INTERESTING SIGHT	DIFFERENCE IN HEIGHT
OBSERVATION **TOWER**	CLIMB 420 M DESCENT 440 M

 **5.2%** ALCOHOL CONTENT

BLONDE
NON-FILTERED
AND BOTTOM-
FERMENTED

 **GOLDEN
YELLOW**

 FRESH

 **REFRESHING
AND ACRID**

BITTERNESS   SWEETNESS

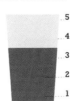 

DESCRIPTION OF THE JOURNEY

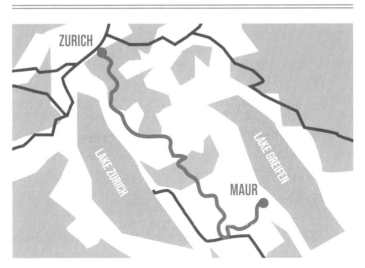

Maur (460 m) → Loorenchopf (694 m) → Chlösterli
→ Schwamendingen (435 m)

At the last tram stop on the Klusplatz in Zurich, take
bus number 747 and get off at the bus stop in the
village of Maur. The bus stop is right in front of the
hiking sign. You can also take bus number 743 from
the train station in Stettach to Maur Dorf and continue
in the direction of the bus until the post office, where

you will need to turn right in order to find the hiking sign.

Take the hiking trail that climbs in the direction of Aesch and cross the ravine. At the bus stop Im Brünneli, leave the trail and go up the Langacherstrasse. After two bends, it leads to the Wassbergstrasse, where you get back onto the hiking trail. Follow the trail in the direction of Forch. After walking through a meadow and then a forest, you arrive at the Forch Denkmal (a memorial site). Here, follow the path in the direction of Süessblätz, where you continue on in the direction of Allmend Fluntern before reaching Loorenchopf.

At Lorrenchopf, there is a picnic area with a fountain and an observation tower.

From here, go in the direction of Chlösterli / Zoo. When at the zoo, take the path in the direction of Schwamendingen. Go along the fence of the zoo and cross over a bridge, which takes you to the forest. Once you have crossed the forest, you will have the opportunity to admire the view of Schwamendingen. On a clear day, you can see the Säntis. After a few meters, turn left at the restaurant Wirtschaft Ziegelhütte, where you can enjoy a Bier Paul in the garden or comfortably seated in the dining room of the restaurant.

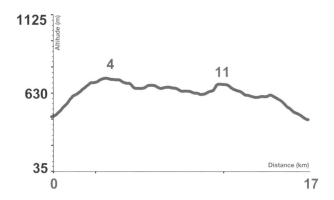

RETURN

Take the footpath for 10 minutes until the Schwamendingerplatz (bus numbers 63 and 94 for Oerlikon, tram number 7 for the main station and the train station Stettbach).

WIRTSCHAFT ZIEGELHÜTTE
Hüttenkopfstrasse 70
8051 Zurich
044 322 40 03
www.wirtschaft-ziegelhuette.ch

BIER PAUL
Brauerei Erusbacher & Paul
Büttikerstrasse 3
5612 Villmergen
056 621 11 00
www.bierpaul.ch

INTERESTING SIGHTS
- The observation tower
- Zurich Zoo
  www.zoo.ch

MEILEN

PANORAMIC TRAIL IN THE PFANNENSTIL

ZH

STARTING POINT	DESTINATION
ZURICH REHALP	**MEILEN**
BEER	DIFFICULTY
USTERBRÄU	**HIKE**
MAP	
SHEEP 225 (ZURICH)	LENGTH OF THE HIKE
SHEEP 226 (RAPPERSWIL) OR THE PANORAMIC TRAIL BROCHURE (WWW.ZPP.CH)	**3H15, 13KM**
INTERESTING SIGHT	DIFFERENCE IN HEIGHT
LAKE RUMEN	CLIMB 200 M DESCENT 300 M

5.0% ALCOHOL CONTENT

BLONDE NON-FILTERED NATURALLY CLOUDY

 GOLDEN YELLOW

 FRESH

 REFRESHING, TANGY

ORIGINAL

USTERBRÄU

BITTERNESS   **SWEETNESS**

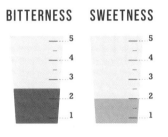

DESCRIPTION OF THE JOURNEY

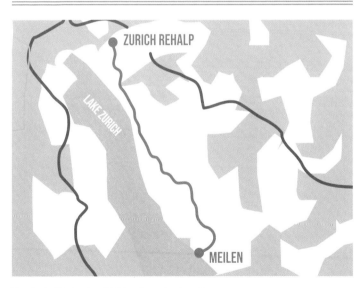

Zurich Rehalp (524 m) → Lake Rumensee
→ Schübelweiher → Küsnachter Tobel → Luft
→ Meilen Fährhafen (406 m)

Take tram number 11 from Zurich's central station to
get to the Rehalp.

This hike has a specific sign. The trail is very easy to follow all the way. The trail brochure is largely sufficient to find your way. It can be downloaded from Pfannenstil's website Zürcher Planungsgruppe (planning group of Zurich).

Shortly past the Rehalp, there is a splendid view of Lake Zurich and the Alps. You can enjoy this view during most of the hike. is only obstructed when walking through the forest or passing behind a house. A short distance after Lake Rumen and the Schübelweiher pond, cross the ravine called Küsnachter Tobel. This is the only steep part of the entire hike. In the summer, this passage is pleasantly cool. But in winter, it can be covered with ice.

At Luft, which overlooks Meilen (a restaurant is noted in the brochure, but it has closed for good), leave the panoramic trail and take the fork leading to the station of Meilen. Take the passage under the platforms and follow the hiking trail in the direction of the boats and ferries. You can try a Usterbräu beer, which comes from the Braukultur brewery, at the kiosk of the last ferry stop.

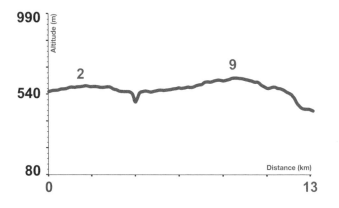

FÄHRENKIOSK MEILEN
Seestrasse 570
8706 Meilen/ZH
044 923 13 20

GOLDKÜSTENBRÄU
Brauereistrasse 16
8610 Uster
044 201 06 09
www.braukultur.ch

INTERESTING SIGHTS
- Lake Rumensee
- The pond Schübelweiher
- The ravine Küsnachter Tobel

MENDRISIOTTO

THE MOST SOUTHERN SWISS BEER

TI

STARTING POINT	DESTINATION
CHIASSO	**STABIO**

BEER	DIFFICULTY
SAN MARTINO	**HIKE**

MAP	
SHEET 296 (CHIASSO)	LENGTH OF THE HIKE
SHEET 286 (MALCANTONE)	**3H15, 12KM**

INTERESTING SIGHT	
THE OLD TICINO HOUSES IN **NOVAZZANO**	DIFFERENCE IN HEIGHT
	CLIMB 410 M DESCENT 290 M

5.2% ALCOHOL CONTENT

NON-FILTERED
NATURALLY
CLOUDY
AND BOTTOM-
FERMENTED

 ORANGE

 LEMON, HONEY, BUTTER

 MALTY

BITTERNESS   SWEETNESS

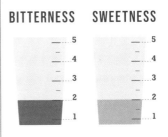

DESCRIPTION OF THE JOURNEY

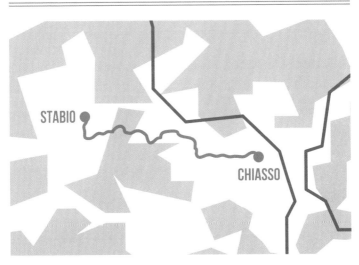

Chiasso (238 m) → Bresciano → Novazzano
→ Monte Morello (495 m) → Brusata → Santa Margherita
→ Stabio (348 m)

From the station in Chiasso, follow the hiking trail in
the direction of Novazzano, via the passage under the
platforms. At the next underground passage, turn
right. Walking along a neighborhood street, follow the
foot of a hill until the path turns left into the woods.

After a short climb, the trail goes up and down through a beautiful mixed forest.

At the intersection, there is no sign indicating the direction to Novazzano. Here, go in the direction of Brescia until the bus stop Ponte Faloppia, where the direction Novazzano is once again indicated. After about 200 meters, there are two paths leading to Novazzano. Turn left to take the shortest one (25 minutes).

Traveling along a sunken lane through the woods, meadows and vineyards, you will come the old village center of Novazzano, where three hiking trails meet up. The marker indicating the direction to take is not visible. Follow the biking trail (red sign, white arrow) until the next hiking signpost and then follow the path in the direction of Brusata. After walking along a small, narrow street lined with old Ticino houses and then a newer neighborhood, you will arrive in Casate, at the foot of Monte Morello.

A steep path with several steps goes through the forest to the summit.

Just before the descent towards Brusata, it's worth continuing on the route for a few more meters to take in the view of some of the high Valais summits through a gap in the wooded hills.

In Brusata, continue until Prella and then until Stabio S. Margherita. The path winds through the forest and the vineyards.

From time to time, you catch a glimpse of Monte Rosa and other summits of the Mischabel massif. In Stabio S. Margherita, continue until Grotto Santa Margherita, where you can have a beer from the local brewery Birrificio Ticino in the shaded garden or comfortably seated at the bar.

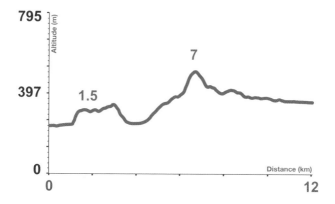

RETURN

You need to return to the last marker and from there go in the direction of Stabio-Paese until the bus stop Stabio Dazio Vecchio. It is a 15 minute walk from the Grotto to the bus stop. At the moment, the trail goes through a large construction site. You must therefore expect some changes and detours. From Dazio Vecchio, buses go to the station in Mendrisio.

GROTTO OSTERIA SANTA MARGHERITA
091 647 33 77

BIRRIFICIO TICINESE
Via Vite 5
6855 Stabio
091 695 41 90
www.ticinobrewingcompany.ch

INTERESTING SIGHT
· The old Ticino houses in Novazzano

MICHAELS-KREUZ

A RANGE OF HILLS WITH BEAUTIFUL PANORAMIC VIEWS IN THE SURROUNDINGS OF LUCERNE

LU

STARTING POINT	**DESTINATION**
GISIKON-ROOT	**LUCERNE**
BEER	**DIFFICULTY**
RATHAUSBIER	
MAP	**HIKE**
SHEET 235	
(ROTKREUZ)	**LENGTH OF THE HIKE**
INTERESTING SIGHT	**4H45, 17KM**
KAPELLBRÜCKE	**DIFFERENCE IN HEIGHT**
(COVERED WOODEN FOOTBRIDGE)	CLIMB 600 M DESCENT 590 M

5.0% ALCOHOL CONTENT NON-FILTERED NATURALLY CLOUDY

 GOLDEN-YELLOW

 LIGHTLY FRUITY

 TANGY

BITTERNESS   SWEETNESS

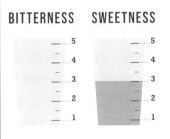

DESCRIPTION OF THE JOURNEY

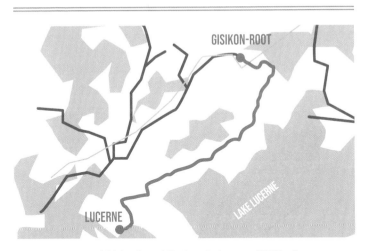

Gisikon-Root (421 m) → Michaelskreuz (795 m)
→ Udligenswil → Adligenswil → Dietschiberg
→ Lucerne (436 m)

You get to Gisikon-Root by taking the train that links
Rotkreuz to Lucerne.

From the station, take the trail in the direction of
Michaelskreuz. At the first intersection, shortly after
the station, the direction is indicated on a white
road sign.

You soon get to the last houses and climb a steep slope through the meadows.

At pt. 624, the hiking trail meets up with a road that you follow to the left until the next group of houses. There, take a hiking trail to the right. The marker, painted on the corner of a house, isn't easy to see. Next, walk up through a meadow. A drinking trough is buried at ground level on the trail. When you see it, you're almost already in the water.

Cross the forest, go by a farm and you will arrive at the Michaelskreuz inn, where you can find the regional mineral water (the Knuttwiler).

On a nice day, it is worth making a detour to the top of the hill behind the restaurant.The view is magnificent. From Michaelskreuz, follow the Alpenpanoramaweg, the panoramic trail of the Alps, in the direction of Lucerne. It is marked with the number 3 on a green background of the yellow signs. It takes you across the range of hills to Udligenswil and then to Adligenswil before arriving on the Dietschiberg and leading down to the lake. Turn right here and walk on the lakeside trail of Lucerne until Seebrücke. Cross the road and walk along the edge of the Reuss River. Pass the Kapellbrücke (the Chapel Bridge, a famous wooden bridge with a tower) and you arrive at the restaurant Rathaus, where the Rathausbier is brewed and served.

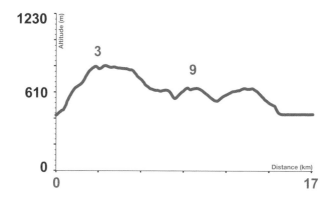

RETURN

From the restaurant Rathaus, follow the river's edge for a short distance. Cross the footbridge Rathaus-Steg and then turn left to the station. This will take 10–15 minutes.

GASTHAUS MICHAELSKREUZ
041 450 11 82
www.gasthausmichaelskreuz.ch

RATHAUS
Unter der Egg 2
6004 Luzern
www.braui-luzern.ch

INTERESTING SIGHTS
- The Kapellbrücke (covered wooden footbridge)
- The old town of Lucerne

NIESEN

HIGH ABOVE LAKE THUN

BE

STARTING POINT	DESTINATION
WIMMIS	**NIESEN**

BEER	DIFFICULTY
RUGENBRÄU	**ALPINE HIKE**

MAP	
SHEET 253	LENGTH OF THE ALPINE HIKE
(GANTRISCH)	**5H30, 9KM**

INTERESTING SIGHT	DIFFERENCE IN HEIGHT
THE NIESENBAHN RACK RAILWAY	CLIMB 1730 M DESCENT 15 M

4.8% ALCOHOL CONTENT

BLONDE FILTERED AND BOTTOM-FERMENTED

 PALE GOLD

 STRAW

LIGHT, FRUITY

BITTERNESS	SWEETNESS
5 4 3 2 1	5 4 3 2 1

DESCRIPTION OF THE JOURNEY

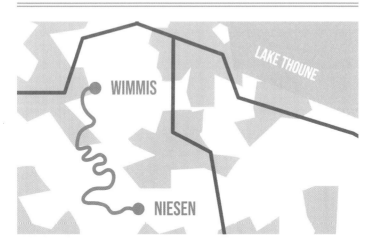

WIMMIS

LAKE THOUNE

NIESEN

Wimmis (629 m) → Niesen (2362 m)

You get to Wimmis by taking the train that links Spiez to Zweisimmen. There are also non-stop trains from Bern (be sure to get on the right car).

The trail from Wimmis to Niesen is so well indicated that a more detailed description isn't necessary. The slope is so steady and pleasant that you climb the 1700 meters more easily than other hikes that are shorter. Furthermore, if you begin early enough, in the summer there is shade during the majority of the hike.

The mountain pasture Ahorni (1565 meters) has a picnic area, from where you can enjoy the view to the north. You may be lucky enough to see llamas because this is where they graze in the summer.

Then continue on the side of the mountain and along the ridge. Thanks to the difference in altitude, the types of flowers along the trail's edge are very diverse. The panoramic view at the summit stretches from the high summits of the Bernese Oberland to the Bernese Pre-alps and to the Jura.

Looking down, you can see Interlaken, where the beer Rugenbräu is brewed. You can drink it at the Gipfel Restaurant.

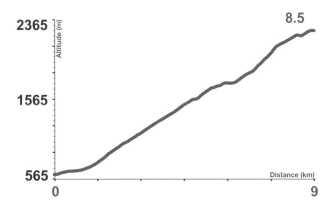

RETURN

Take the rack railway, which is more than 100 years old, in the direction of Mülenen. From there, you can take the train for Spiez, Bern, Brig and Frutigen. During peak periods, the rack railway from Niesen runs every 15 minutes. However, be prepared to wait because of the limited number of seats. The last trip for the valley is at 5:45 pm (summer schedule 2019). Some nights there are additional trains.

NIESEN
Gipfelrestaurant und Bahn
033 676 77 11
www.niesen.ch

RUGENBRÄU
Wagnerenstrasse 40
3800 Matten
033 826 46 46
www.rugenbraeu.ch

INTERESTING SIGHT
- The Niesenbahn, a rack railway over 100 years old

PFAFFHAUSEN

LAKE GREIFEN, A GIFT FROM THE LINTH GLACIER

ZH

STARTING POINT	DESTINATION
NÄNIKON-GREIFENSEE	**GOCKHAUSEN**

BEER	DIFFICULTY
CHOPFAB	**HIKE**

MAP	LENGTH OF THE HIKE
SHEET 226 (RAPPERSWIL) **SHEET 225** (ZURICH)	**5H15, 21 KM**

INTERESTING SIGHT	DIFFERENCE IN HEIGHT
SILBERWEIDE NATURE STATION	CLIMB 370 M DESCENT 250 M

 **5.0%** ALCOHOL CONTENT — CRYSTAL CLEAR TOP-FERMENTED BLONDE

 GOLDEN YELLOW

 HOPPY

 FULL-BODIED

BITTERNESS   SWEETNESS

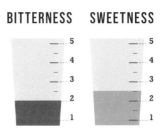

DESCRIPTION OF THE JOURNEY

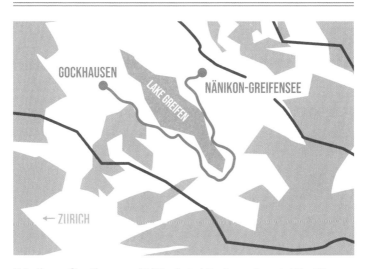

Nänikon-Greifensee (449 m) → Niederuster → Riedikon → Maur → Ebmatingen → Pfaffhausen (614 m) → Geeren → Gockhausen (563 m)

You get to Nänikon-Greifensee by taking the S-Bahn from Zurich.

From the station, follow the hiking trail in the direction of Greifensee. After about 15 minutes, just before the castle, turn left to reach the lakeside hike in the direction of Niederuster Bad. From there, continue on the trail in the direction of Maur. Old trees and reeds grow along the water's edge and there is often a beautiful view of the Alps. Silberweide Nature Station, a nature center popular for birdwatching, is at the far south side of the lake.

In Maur, cross the road that leads down to the pier and continue straight ahead for about 150 meters until the next sign. There, continue on straight ahead in the direction of Ebmatingen. Soon afterwards, the trail climbs diagonally up the slope, passing by the edge of Ebmatingen on the way to Pfaffhausen.

From Pfaffhausen, follow the path to Geeren. After crossing a forest and a large meadow, you'll find yourself at the restaurant Geeren. The restaurant serves a variety of beers, including the two young, regional breweries Chopfab and Usterbräu. Also represented are other larger but still independent breweries, including Müller-Bräu, Sonnenbräu and Appenzeller Bier.

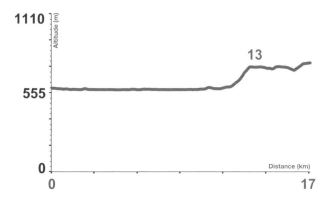

RETURN

From Geeren, follow the path towards Zurich zoo. It's about a 20 minute walk through the forest to an intersection where you turn right to head down to the bus stop called Gockhausen Dorf. Altogether it takes about half an hour. Gockhausen is on the bus route Zurich Fluntern–Stettbach.
You can also reach this bus stop from Geeren by going straight down Obere Geerenstrasse. It's not as pretty, but it's a quarter of an hour shorter.

SHORTCUT

If you start the hike in Riedikon, it's an hour and a half shorter (bus route Uster–Oetwil am See).
If you start the hike in Maur it's three hours shorter (bus connections from Stettbach station and Zurich Klusplatz).

RESTAURANT GEEREN
Obere Geerenstrasse 72
8044 Gockhausen
044821 40 11
www.geeren.ch

BRAUEREI CHOPFAB
Industriestrasse 40
8404 Winterthur
052 233 0870
www.doppelleu.ch

INTERESTING SIGHTS
*   Lake Greifen
*   Silberweide Nature Station

PRAGEL PASS

FROM THE MUOTATHAL THROUGH TO THE KLÖNTAL WITH ITS
CENTENNIAL SPRUCE TREES AND DEEP SINKHOLES

SZ

STARTING POINT	**DESTINATION**
MUOTATHAL HÖLLOCH	**VORDER RICHISAU**
BEER	**DIFFICULTY**
ADLER PANIX-PERLE	**ALPINE HIKE**
MAP	
SHEET 246 (KLAUSEN PASS)	**LENGTH OF THE ALPINE HIKE**
SHEET 236 (LACHEN)	**5H45, 17KM**
INTERESTING SIGHT	**DIFFERENCE IN HEIGHT**
BÖDMERENWALD FOREST, A PRIMEVAL FOREST	**CLIMB 1120 M DESCENT 650 M**

5.2% ALCOHOL CONTENT

BLONDE NON-FILTERED AND BOTTOM-FERMENTED

 STRAW YELLOW

 FRESH

 INTENSE

BITTERNESS   SWEETNESS

DESCRIPTION OF THE JOURNEY

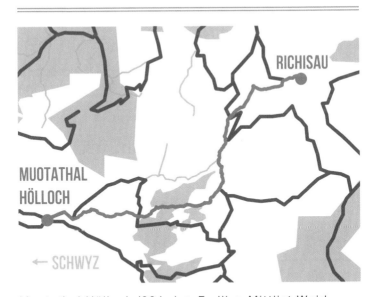

Muotathal Hölloch (664m) → Fedli → Mittlist Weid → Bödmerenwald → Zingel (1736m) → Chalberloch → Pragel → Richisau (1102m)

The entire hike is very well marked with red and white signs, which are however not very frequent. From the bus stop Hölloch, follow the trail in the direction of Gross Band.

You will walk along a road for about 45 minutes. Then, turn right in the direction of Alp Fedli. After the house, take a left in the direction of Pragel. Via the scattered woods and the mountain pastures, you will pass Mittlist Weid and then arrive at Mittenwald.

From there, follow the trail in the direction of Bödmeren. Go through the Bödmerenwald forest with its old spruce trees and deep sinkholes. There is a fork in the middle of the forest. You will see a hand-made marker indicating Riggenloch straight ahead. To the right, there are red and white markers without directions. Regardless, the two trails meet up after the Roggenstöckli. I took the trail to the right. It follows a slightly inclined path through the forest and leads to some limestone formations.

After passing the Roggenstöckli you arrive at the intersection of the four trails. There, follow the red and white sign indicating an easy mountain trail. After about 10 minutes you will come to a mountain refuge with a signpost directing you to Pragel.

Once you've passed the beautiful limestone formations, you arrive on a plateau. Then go down to Pragel Pass. Once at the pass, cross the street and follow the red and white markers in the direction of Alpwirtschaft Pragelpasshöhe. You can take a break there, but you can also buy some cheese or spend the night if you'd like. From this alpine farm, follow the trail in the direction of Vorder Richisau. It only follows the road for the last 800 meters, so you will have a chance to take in the unique panoramic view of the Klöntal. The trail crosses the road sometimes. Please do not cross without looking. It's a popular cycle track.

At the Richisau inn, you can savor the beer Alderbräu in the comfortable inn or in the garden under the shade of the old maple trees.

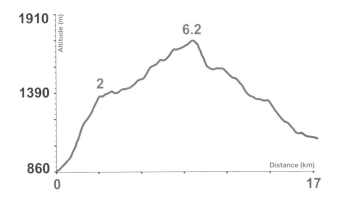

RETURN

To finish the hike, you will enjoy a scenic post bus ride along Lake Klöntal, ending at the station of Glarus.

ALPWIRTSCHAFT PRAGELPASSHÖHE
041 830 12 25

GASTHAUS RICHISAU
055 640 10 85
www.gasthaus-richisau.ch

ADLERBRÄU
Hauptstrasse 34
8762 Schwanden
055 647 35 35
www.brauereiadler.ch

INTERESTING SIGHTS
· Bödmerenwald forest, a primeval forest
· Lake Klöntal

RAPPERSWIL

ON WINDING ROUTES THROUGH A HILLY LANDSCAPE

SG

STARTING POINT	DESTINATION
RÜTI	**RAPPERSWIL**
BEER	DIFFICULTY
XXA INDIAN PALE ALE	**HIKE**
MAP	
SHEET 226	LENGTH OF THE HIKE
(RAPPERSWIL)	**5H15, 21KM**
INTERESTING SIGHT	DIFFERENCE IN HEIGHT
OLD TOWN OF RAPPERSWIL	CLIMB 360 M DESCENT 420 M

4.8% ALCOHOL CONTENT **PALE ALE**

 AMBER

 FRUITY WITH HOPPY NOTES

 BITTER-SWEET

BITTERNESS   SWEETNESS

DESCRIPTION OF THE JOURNEY

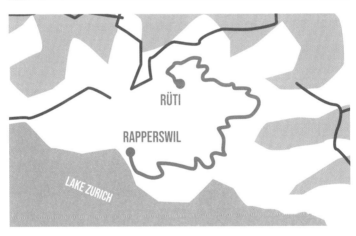

Rüti (482 m) → Tannertobel → Fägswil → Grossweiher
→ Honegg → Chraueren → Lütschbach → Eggwald
→ Chälenstich → Wagen → Ankenloch → Wurmsbach
→ Rapperswil (409 m)

You can reach Rüti on the Zurich S-Bahn. The route
isn't always very well indicated. There are not always
markers. The trail going along the forest above
Fägswil until the route after Grossweiher is not
marked in red on the hiking map (2005 edition).
The station in Rüti has two underpasses, which are

the departure points of several trails. Take the underground passage that is the closest to the kiosk and follow the trail in the direction of Fägswil. You first go through an industrial park and then a recycling center, which is not especially scenic though interesting to see. After 15 minutes, you will enter the wilderness of the Tannertobel. Go up the Jona River, which has sunk deeply into the rock. Then climb a steep slope until a plateau and you arrive in Fägswil.

In Unterfägswil, take the direction of Oberfägswil. Once you pass by a school, turn right onto a trail indicating Grossweiher. At the next farm (where they sell mountain cheese), continue straight ahead. Shortly after, branch off to the right in the direction of Weiher.

After a bend to the left, the trail passes in front of a small nature reserve before reaching the edge of the forest. At the signpost just in front of the forest's edge, leave the trail and take a left, passing a bench just before entering the forest.

Follow the trail until it turns into a paved road. (Here, you can see that you were on a hiking trail because there is a sign which indicates Neu York in the direction from where you came.)

Follow the paved road to the right. Turn left at the next hiking sign and go in the direction of Grossweiher, which isn't a pond, despite its name, but a marsh with some small basins. Walk around the marsh to the right and follow the direction of Niggital until the next intersection, where you follow Widenriet until you come to a paved road. There, turn right in the direction of Eschenbach.

Soon afterwards, you leave the road and go to Chraueren after passing Honegg (still in the direction of Eschenbach). Before crossing the Lattenbach River, you you may wish to make a short detour to the left to see a small waterfall.

After the bridge over the Lattenbach, the trail becomes harder to see. It leads up to a wooden barn at the upper end of the meadow. From there, continue towards Lütschbach (still in the direction of Eschenbach). In the village, turn right, cross a small valley and go up towards Eggwald. Leave this trail going to Eschenbach when you are on the ridge and follow the trail that leads to Chälenstich. From there, cross the road and continue in the direction of Wagen. On a clear day, there is a beautiful view of the Wägital Valley and the surrounding mountains. At Wagen, take the trail going to Wurmsbach. There is no marker in the forest as you arrive at Ankenloch. Turn right. At Wurmsbach, go across the railroad tracks and take the path along the shore until the station in Rapperswil.

At the station in Rapperswil, take the underpass (a map of the city is posted) and then turn right between Avec (a convenience store) and the post office onto Güterstrasse street. Walk until you reach th street Neuen Jonastrasse. Follow this road to the right. Turn right at Eichfeldstrasse and follow it to the end. Go further along Eichwiesstrasse where you'll find the Bier Factory. Check the website for opening hours.

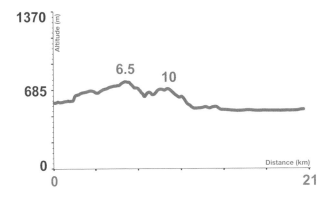

RETURN

There's a bus from Zeughaus back to the Rapperswil train station.

BIER FACTORY RAPPERSWIL
Eichwiesstrasse 6
8645 Rapperswil-Jona
055 210 96 22
www.bierfactory.ch

INTERESTING SIGHTS
* Tannertobel
* The old town of Rapperswil

RHONE

IN THE NATURE RESERVE OF THE RADE AND THE GENEVAN RHONE

STARTING POINT	**DESTINATION**
AIRE-LA-VILLE PONT DE PENEY	**GENEVA** PLACE DU MOLARD
BEER	**DIFFICULTY**
LA MOLARDIÈRE	**HIKE**
MAP	
SHEET 270	**LENGTH OF THE HIKE**
(GENEVA)	**4H, 16KM**
INTERESTING SIGHT	**DIFFERENCE IN HEIGHT**
WATER JET FOUNTAIN	CLIMB 200 M DESCENT 190 M

5.0% ALCOHOL CONTENT

BLONDE
NATURALLY
CLOUDY
TOP-FERMENTED

 PALE GOLD

 AROMATIC LEMONY

 MALTY

BITTERNESS   SWEETNESS

BITTERNESS: 5 4 3 2 1

SWEETNESS: 5 4 3 2 1

DESCRIPTION OF THE JOURNEY

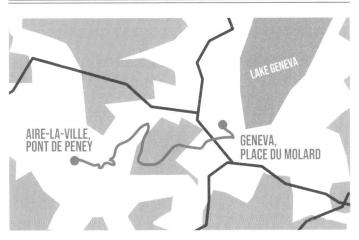

LAKE GENEVA

AIRE-LA-VILLE,
PONT DE PENEY

GENEVA,
PLACE DU MOLARD

Aire-la-Ville, Pont de Peney (375 m) → Le Lignon
→ La Jonction → Geneva, Place du Molard (391 m)

The Pont de Peney bus stop is on the
Satigny-Bernex bus line.

From Pont de Peney, follow the hiking path in the
direction of La Jonction. Depending on the direction
you come from to get to Pont de Peney, you will find
yourself on one side or the other of a traffic circle. The
signpost is located on the south-west side of the road.

From the traffic circle, follow the road for about 500 meters, heading south-east parallel to the Rhone River. Then the road curves to the right and the path continues up the river.

The path is well marked and mostly leads you through a beautiful broad-leaved forest on the steep banks of the Rhone. There's not a single house in sight. The sounds are the only reminder that the town is nearby. This region is very important for waterfowl and migrating birds.

Below Saint-Georges, the Arve River flows into the Rhone. Here, go down the slope diagonally until you reach the bridge. Cross the Arve and carry on until you get to the La Jonction tram stop, which marks the end of the hiking path. Keep going in the same direction as before until you get back to the banks of the Rhone. Take a right here and you will soon find yourself away from the traffic, on a boardwalk ideal for strolling along.

Follow the Rhone until you reach the landing pier at the Quai du Général Guisan, just before the Mont-Blanc bridge.

There is a city map at this point. Take a right and go past the the old Tour du Molard to get to la place du Molard (Molard square). Cross the square diagonally to arrive at the Brasserie du Molard (Molard Brewery). I particularly like the fact that you can order a tasting tray with a variety of beers from the brewery.

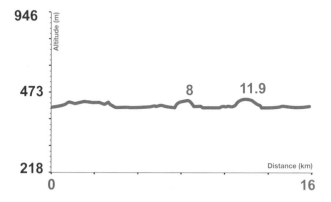

RETURN

Go back up to the Quai du Général-Guisan and then onto the Pont du Mont-Blanc to go to the station. It should take about 15 minutes to get there. The rocks in the harbor next to the Jet d'Eau are called les Pierres du Niton (Neptune's stones) and are the reference point for the Swiss national height measurement system.

BRASSERIE DU MOLARD
Place du Molard 9
1204 Genève
022 311 11 00
www.brasseriedumolard.ch

INTERESTING SIGHTS
- The Molard Tower
- Jet d'Eau (Water jet fountain)
- Pierres du Niton (Neptune's stones)

ROGGENSTOCK

A MARSH, A SULFUR SPRING AND A GORGE WITH WHITE WALLS

SZ

STARTING POINT	DESTINATION
OBERIBERG	**OBERIBERG**

BEER	DIFFICULTY
MAISGOLD	**ALPINE HIKE**

MAP	
SHEET 236	LENGTH OF THE ALPINE HIKE
(LACHEN)	**4H30, 11KM**

INTERESTING SIGHT	DIFFERENCE IN HEIGHT
THE MINSTER GORGE	**CLIMB AND DESCENT 720 M**

5.0% ALCOHOL CONTENT

BLONDE BOTTOM-FERMENTED

 PALE GOLD

 FRUITY, WITH A HINT OF APPLE

 LIGHT TOUCH OF HAZELNUT

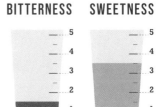

BITTERNESS   SWEETNESS

DESCRIPTION OF THE JOURNEY

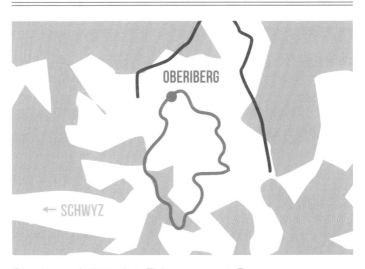

OBERIBERG

← SCHWYZ

Oberiberg (1087 m) → Tubenmoos → Roggenegg
→ Roggenstock (1777 m) → Roggenhütte → Fuederegg
→ Tschalun → Oberiberg

You get to Oberiberg by taking the post bus from
Einsiedeln

The hiking signpost isn't directly at the post office, but
instead a few meters further at the intersection. Follow

the road for a short distance in the same direction. Then, turn right onto a trail going in the direction of Roggenstock. At Moos, you emerge onto a street that you climb up. Shortly before the ski-lifts, the road forks. Here, don't go to the right in the direction of Roggenstock, go towards Alderhorst instead. A little later, in a ravine, the trail branches to the right. Walk along a stream and then cross a meadow. You will come to a street leading to Tubenmoss. A nice path crosses the marshes and mountain farms of Roggenegg.

The rest of the trail isn't marked. Walk on the ridge, which begins above the mountain refuge, until you see an orange signpost in the bushes. From there on, you will be on a scenic and steep path. It veers onto the right slope once and stays on the ridge the rest of the time. It takes half an hour to go from Roggenegg to Roggenstock.

The descent is once again indicated with red and white markers. Walk down the ridge until you reach the pass, after which the trail follows an arc through the Ober Roggen mountain pasture until the refuge of Roggen. A wide path then leads to the mountain restaurant Fuederegg. On the road, you will walk by the hotel Skihaus / Skihus and continue until you cross a ravine. Next to the ravine there is an unmarked trail going down to the right. After a few meters, turn right on the trail in the direction of the waterfall with the sulfur spring. You get back to Fuederegg the same way.

This loops takes half an hour (this time is counted in the length of the hike).

At Fuederegg, follow the road in the direction of Oberiberg until the forest. Just before the bridge to the left, you can see a small gravel parking lot. This is where the trail branches off in the direction of Oberiberg.

When I was looking for markers, one was easily seen on a tree; however, it also has a marker of another color, which can make things a little confusing. Once you've found the start of the path, there's no risk of taking the wrong trail. Continue along the slope and cross the road that goes from Fuederegg to Oberiberg. You leave the forest at Guggeli.

By continuing on this road, you will come to Gütschli. From there, do not go directly to Oberiberg. Instead, take a left onto the road. Follow the road for a short distance before turning onto a path in the direction of Tschalun. There, cross the main road and follow the path in the direction of Minsterschlucht (Minster gorge). First, you pass through narrow local streets and then go along the Minster to arrive in the narrow gorge that the river carved into the white cliffs.

Unfortunately, the path in the gorge is not open because of possible falling rocks. You can however enjoy a view from the top of the gorge.

From the gorge, climb up across a meadow until the main road which you follow until the post office, about 10 minutes away.
In Oberiberg, several restaurants serve the beer Maisgold from the Einsiedler brewery.

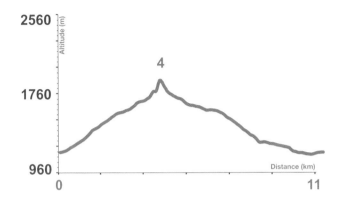

ALPWIRTSCHAFT ROGGENEGG
055 414 25 05

BERGRESTAURANT FUEDEREGG
055 414 16 83
www.fuederegg.ch

EINSIEDLER BIER
Brauerei Rosengarten AG
Spitalstrasse 14
8840 Einsiedeln
055 418 86 86
www.einsiedlerbier.ch

INTERESTING SIGHTS
- The marsh of Tubenmoos
- The waterfall with a sulfur spring
- The Minster gorge

ROTSTEIN PASS

FROM THE APPENZELL REGION TO TOGGENBURG

STARTING POINT

WASSERAUEN

BEER

SÄNTISBIER

MAP

SHEET 227

(APPENZELL)

INTERESTING SIGHT

MOUNTAIN GOATS OF ROTSTEIN PASS

DESTINATION

GAMPLÜT

DIFFICULTY

ALPINE HIKE

LENGTH OF THE ALPINE HIKE

6H30, 15KM

DIFFERENCE IN HEIGHT

CLIMB 1430 M
DESCENT 940 M

5.2% ALCOHOL CONTENT

**BLONDE
NON-FILTERED
NATURALLY
CLOUDY**

 GOLDEN BLONDE

 FLOWERY

 INTENSE

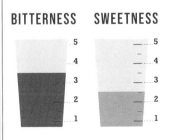

BITTERNESS   SWEETNESS

DESCRIPTION OF THE JOURNEY

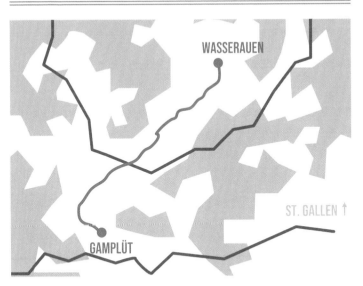

Wasserauen (872 m) → Schrennen → Meglisalp
→ Rotsteinpass (2120 m) → Langenbüel
→ Gamplüt (1357 m)

You can get to Wasserauen by taking the Appenzell
train (Appenzellerbahn) from Gossau. The entire
route is very well marked, but the time estimations
on the markers are contradictory. Follow the road for

a few meters while climbing up the valley. Then turn left in the direction of Meglisalp (via Schrennen) – Rotsteinpass. You will cross a forest and some mountain pastures, then a steep slope between rocky outcrops high over Lake Seealpsee. A small refuge in the steep slope has a shelter in case of an emergency. After a short descent, you get to the Meglisalp mountain inn (rooms and dormitories). You then pass Oberschelen to reach the Rotstein Pass. Here, there is also a mountain inn for lodging.
Its terrace offers a magnificent view, and with a little luck you will see some mountain goats.
To go back down, follow the road until Wildhaus, passing by Schafboden (a guest house with a bar and dormitories) and then Langenbüel. Several bends along the journey provide wonderful view of the Alpstein cliffs and Toggenburg mountains.
In Langenbüel, take the path in the direction of Gamplüt. It passes through a forest above Thurwies then leads slightly uphill to Gamplüt.
At the entrance sign of Gamplüt (1350 meters), walk about 100 meters to the right to get to the upper cable car station of Wildhaus, where you will find the Gamplüt restaurant. This restaurant serves beer from the Schützengarten brewery of St. Gallen.

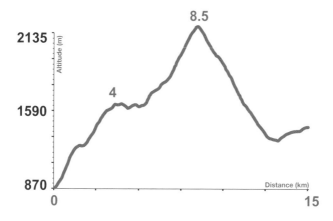

RETURN

Take the cable car to Wildhaus. From the lower station, it takes 10 minutes to get to the post office where you'll find the post bus line Buchs–Nesslau–Neu St. Johann. You need to check the cable car hours because if you miss the last one, it takes 35 minutes by foot to get to the post office in Wildhaus.

BERGGASTHAUS MEGLISALP
071 799 11 28
www.meglisalp.ch

ROTSTEINPASS
071 799 11 41
www.rotsteinpass.ch

SCHAFBODEN
071 999 13 45

BERGRESTAURANT UND GONDELBAHN
Gamplüt
071 999 21 72
www.gampluet.ch

BRAUEREI SCHÜTZENGARTEN
St. Jakob-Strasse 37
Postfach 63
9004 St. Gallen
071 243 43 43
www.schuetzengarten.ch

INTERESTING SIGHT
- The mountain goats of Rotstein Pass

SARINE

SHADED TRAIL ON THE BANKS OF TWO RIVERS

FR

STARTING POINT	DESTINATION
MARLY GÉRINE	**POSIEUX**
BEER	DIFFICULTY
LA ROUSSE CROIX-BLANCHE	**ALPINE HIKE**
MAP	
SHEET 252	LENGTH OF THE ALPINE HIKE
(BULLE)	**2H45, 11KM**
INTERESTING SIGHT	DIFFERENCE IN HEIGHT
THE NOUTES RAMP	CLIMB 240 M
HISTORIC ROUTE IN MARLY	DESCENT 180 M

5.0% ALCOHOL CONTENT

AMBER
NON-FILTERED
TOP-FERMENTED

 AMBER

 APRICOT
SPECULOOS

 CARAMEL

BITTERNESS

5
4
3
2
1

SWEETNESS

5
4
3
2
1

DESCRIPTION OF THE JOURNEY

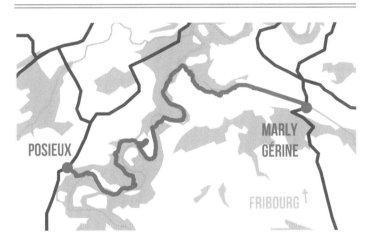

Marly Gérine (618m) → Abbaye d'Hauterive
→ Posieux (681m)

You get to Marly Gérine by taking bus number 1 from the station in Fribourg. The bus stop is at Place de la Gare and not in the underground bus station.

From Marly Gérine, follow the marked trail towards the Abbey of Hauterive. The Abbey isn't mentioned on all the signs. The signs indicate sometimes Au Port or 700 Anniversaire. Always stay on the left bank of the

Gérine (in the same direction as the current). At first, the river is the river is channeled and built into sills, but soon afterwards it winds on gravel beds and around small islands. The path passes through a narrow stretch of forest directly on the edge of the river until a steep bank.

From there, climb up and take a narrow trail to cross a steep slope where you must be surefooted. After a short descent, you arrive at the confluence of the Gérine and the Sarine. From here, you will walk along the Sarine. The trail forks from time to time into several beaten paths.

If you feel disoriented, use the river bank to guide you. Here too, it winds between beds of gravel and bushes and is channeled only near a plant. Shortly after, cross the Sarine and continue on the other bank. You will walk around the Abbey of Hauterive, which was built in a loop of the Sarine.

The opposite bank is a rock face, vertical and smooth. You arrive at a bridge and go to the right, on the hiking trail towards Posieux. You will pass in front of the entrance to a cloister. A section of the trail climbs in the form of an arc until you get to an intersection. There, stop following Posieux and take the Circuit Hauterive via the forest.

At the next intersection, continue on the Circuit Hauterive in the direction of la Tuffière. You will soon find yourself on a bank where the trail winds through bushes, under a rocky overhang and between boulders from an old mountain landslide. Next, you pass a meadow and arrive at the next fork. Here again, don't go directly towards Posieux. Instead, continue for about 5 minutes in the direction of la Tuffière, until you see a large hiking signpost on your right indicating Au village par la fontaine. Take a right and climb up to the forest on a trail with wooden steps. The trail divides at the edge of the forest. Turn right and you will arrive on the main road of Posieux. Cross the road diagonally to the left in order to get to the La Croix Blanche brewery.

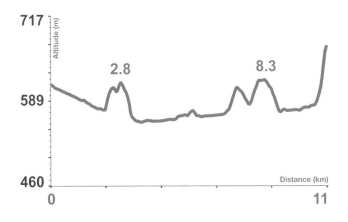

RETURN

The village of Posieux is on the bus line Bulle–
Fribourg. To go to Bulle, board the bus right beside La
Croix Blanche. For Fribourg, the stop is 400 meters
to the left.

BRASSERIE LA CROIX-BLANCHE
Rte de Fribourg 71
1725 Posieux
026 411 99 00
www.brasserie-fribourg.com

SALPETERHÖHLE

THROUGH THE GORGES OF THE WISSBACH AND GLATT RIVERS

SG

STARTING POINT	**DESTINATION**
# DEGERSHEIM	# GOSSAU
BEER	**DIFFICULTY**
FREIHOF BEER	**ALPINE HIKE**
MAP	
# SHEET 227	**LENGTH OF THE ALPINE HIKE**
(APPENZELL)	# 4H30, 15KM
INTERESTING SIGHT	**DIFFERENCE IN HEIGHT**
LAKE ISENHAMMER THE FLOOD PLAIN	CLIMB 400 M DESCENT 560 M

4.8% ALCOHOL CONTENT

BLONDE
NON-FILTERED
BOTTOM-
FERMENTED

 GOLDEN YELLOW

 MALTY, HINT OF CITRUS

 INTENSE

LAGER BIER

BITTERNESS	SWEETNESS
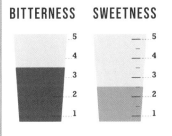	

DESCRIPTION OF THE JOURNEY

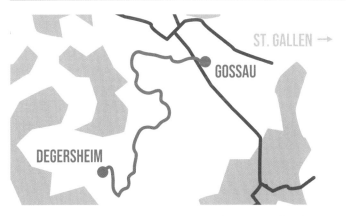

ST. GALLEN →

GOSSAU

DEGERSHEIM

Degersheim (799 m) → Fuchsacker (969 m) → Büel
→ Talmühle → Wissbachschlucht → Schwänberg
→ Salpeterhöhle → Ruine Helfenberg → Höfrig
→ Niderdorf → Brauerei Freihof → Gossau (638 m)

Degersheim is on the Lucerne–Roamnshorn
(Voralpenexpress) railroad line.

From the station, follow the path that climbs to the
restaurant Fuchsacker. After about 10 minutes,
there are two paths that go to Fuchsacker. Take a left
there. You reach the ridge after walking around a big

arc. From Fuchsacker, walk down to Tal via Büel. The restaurant Kantonsgrenze is just off the road. Cross the road and head straight on in the direction of Talmuhle (road sign for cars direction Flawil, Egg).

When you get to Talmuhle, turn right and follow the path in the direction of Schwänberg. This leads to a barn, then across a meadow till you get to a picnic area near the Wissbach River. Follow the Wissbach through the forest. The river disappears suddenly into a crevice.

The path continues along a wooden footbridge. On the rock face opposite you, you can see a giant basin carved out by a whirlpool. As you walk farther down, the Wissbach is calm again and there are pebble beaches where children splash about in the summer. After a few bends, climb up to Schwändberg and from there go down to Tobelmüli.

At Tobelmüli, follow the path in the direction of Rüti. Cross the Glatt River and then begin a gentle climb until you reach a sharp right turn in the path. Here, follow the path towards the Salpeterhöhle cave (red markings). This is an unmarked path. It is narrow and slopes steeply through the woods.

When the path is wet, it becomes slippery. After about 15 minutes of climbing up and down through the bushes, you will spot the entrance to the cave. It is closed because of a risk that it might collapse. Nonetheless, it is interesting to see from the outside. Pass the cave and walk down along the river.

Here, the Glatt flows through a virgin forest. The path is flat at first as it follows the shoreline. Then it climbs for a short distance until you get to an area with a barbecue pit. Several dirt trails meet up here.

One of them has wooden steps and climbs up to the right.

Climb about 100 meters along this trail. After that, the ground is flatter and you get back onto the hiking trail going from Rüti to the ruins of Helfenberg. Take a left you will see a yellow marker after a short distance.

From the ruins of Helfenberg, follow the path in the direction of Hüfrig (indicated on the maps as Höfrig or Stadtwald). This path is a steep slope down to the Glatt River. It then crosses a picturesque valley, passes under a railroad viaduct and continues to the former Lake Isenhammer. This artificial lake was removed in the summer of 2012. Now, there is an alluvial plain that provides shelter for many rare animals.

After Isenhammer, part of the Glatt flows into a narrow crevice on the right of the path. The other part of the river flows into a factory canal on the left of the path. Go across the crevice, then cross a road and continue the hike in the direction of Höfrig.

At the edge of the forest, there are two paths that lead

to Gossau. Take the path to the right, which is the most direct.

This leads to a plateau with a view of Mount Säntis.

Soon you will see a brick building with big windows and a flat roof. This is the Freihof brewery.

The path leads to the Flawilerstrasse. Leave the path at this point and another few steps will take you to the brewery.

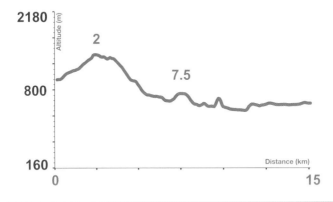

RETURN

Go back to the hiking path and follow it to Gossau station. It will take you about 20 minutes. If you want to go westward by train, you will have to cross the Glatt. If you look out of the window to the right (in the same direction that the train is traveling), you will see the Isenhammer alluvial plain.

BERGGASTHAUS FUCHSACKER
071 371 11 66
www.fuchsacker.ch

FREIHOF BRAUEREI & HOFSTUBE
Flawilerstrasse 46
9201 Gossau/SG
071 385 34 34
www.freihofag.ch

INTERESTING SIGHTS
- The Salpeterhöhle (Salpeter cave)
- The ruins of Helfenberg castle
- Lake Isenhammer and the alluvial plain

SIHLSPRUNG

THROUGH A NARROW GORGE IN A VAST LANDSCAPE OF DRUMLINS

ZH

STARTING POINT	DESTINATION
NEUHEIM TAL	**WÄDENSWIL**

BEER	DIFFICULTY
WÄDI-BRÄU	**HIKE**

MAP

SHEET 235 (ROTKREUZ)
SHEET 236 (LACHEN)
SHEET 226 (RAPPERSWIL)

LENGTH OF THE HIKE

3H30, 13KM

INTERESTING SIGHT

LANDSCAPE OF DRUMLINS

DIFFERENCE IN HEIGHT

CLIMB 250 M
DESCENT 440 M

4.8% ALCOHOL CONTENT

BLONDE NON-FILTERED NATURALLY CLOUDY

 GOLDEN YELLOW

 SPICY

 SPICED

BITTERNESS

— 5
— 4
— 3
— 2
— 1

SWEETNESS

— 5
— 4
— 3
— 2
— 1

DESCRIPTION OF THE JOURNEY

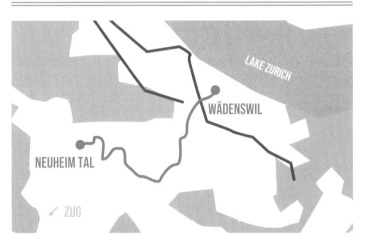

LAKE ZURICH

WÄDENSWIL

NEUHEIM TAL

ZUG

Tal (600 m) → Sihlsprung → Sihlmatt → Suener
→ Neubad → Schönenberg → Herrlisberg
→ Wädenswil (408 m)

Tal is on the post bus line Baar–Neuheim.

In the event of rain or thawing, the path crossing
Sihlsprung can be declared inaccessible because of
falling rocks or ice. At the bus stop Tal, follow the
hiking path in the direction of Sihlsprung–Sihlmatt.
It leads to Sihl after passing the farm Sennweid. From

there, go up the river on either bank until Sihlsprung. If you take the left bank, you won't see the most beautiful section of the trail because the path passes through a tunnel there.

That's why I recommend taking the trail that goes by the covered wooden bridge and then the right bank. The valley narrows and the rock faces become steeper. At Sihlsprung, the Sihl river has cleared a trail into a narrow gorge.

By passing a bridge and some short tunnels, you get to Sihlmatt where the valley broadens once again. Cross the Sihl again via the Suenerstäg bridge and follow the path in the direction of Schönenberg. Climb uphill. You will come upon a landscape of large drumlins. Cross a small marsh to get to Schönenberg, where you have to follow the trail in the direction of Herrlisberg–Wädenswil. At Herrlisberg, cross the highway and a little after that there is a lovely view of Wädenswil and Lake Zurich. The trail becomes steeper and goes down to Wädenswil, after going through some fields. Stay on the same trail until you get to the church.

Here, leave the trail and turn left after passing the church. Just after the bus stop Sonnenstrasse, you will come to a crossroads.

You have to cross the street Zugerstrasse and continue on the street Florhofstrasse until the Wädi-Brau-Huus brewery.

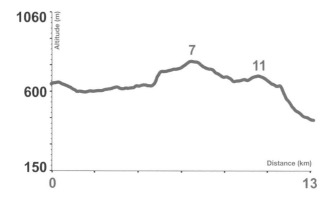

RETURN

Return to the street Zugerstrasse and follow it to the station. It takes 15 minutes to get to the station from the Wädi-Brau-Huus brewery.

RESTAURANT SIHLMATT
041 755 12 44
www.sihlmatt.ch

WÄDI-BRAU-HUUS
Florhofstrasse 13, "di alt Fabrik"
Postfach
8820 Wädenswil
044 783 93 92
www.waedenswiler.ch

INTERESTING SIGHTS
* Sihlsprung, a gorge
* The landscape of drumlins

STAMMHEIM

PONDS, LAKES AND A RIVER NORTH OF WINTERTHUR

ZH

STARTING POINT	DESTINATION
SEUZACH	**STAMMHEIM**
BEER	DIFFICULTY
HÖPFEN BRÄU	**HIKE**
MAP	
SHEET 216 (FRAUENFELD)	LENGTH OF THE HIKE
	5H, 21KM
INTERESTING SIGHT	DIFFERENCE IN HEIGHT
EDUCATIONAL TRAIL	CLIMB 270 M DESCENT 290 M

NATURALLY
CLOUDY

 DARK BLONDE

 SPICY

 REFRESHING

BITTERNESS   SWEETNESS

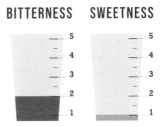

DESCRIPTION OF THE JOURNEY

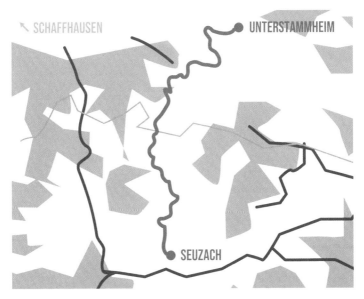

Seuzach (455 m) → Weier* → Gurisee* → Buecher Weier*
→ Rümbeli* → Berg → Gütighausen → Thur
→ Barchetsee → Waltalingen → Guntalingen
→ Stammheim (433 m)

* These lakes are all indicated on the 1/50 000 map, but their names are not.

Seuzach is on the Winterthur–Stein am Rhein railroad line that you will cross several times during this hike. You will find the hiking signs in the passages that pass under the platforms at the station. Take the path towards Weier–Gurisee–Andelfingen.

The path begins by running alongside the railroad track until you get to Weier. Then walk through the fields and go through Bänk and Welsikon before arriving at Lake Guri (a marsh of national value).

A short distance into the forest, you will come to some reeds. One path goes to the right and another to the left, but no direction is indicated on either side. Take the left path.

Soon, you will catch sight of a lake with water lilies and lots of other aquatic plants. If it's the right season, you may also hear a symphony of frogs.

At the northernmost point of the lake, there is a wonderful picnic area.

The path carries on to Buecher Weier pond and then goes through Rümbeli before reaching the road that runs between Niederwil and Gütighausen. From then on, follow the hiking path going in the direction of Gütighausen–Barchetsee–Stammheim. Follow this road for a short while and then leave the road to the left. Walk under the railroad track to get to Gütighausen. Walk through the village and then cross the Thur River. After that, go under the bridge and down the river for about 500 meters. At the inn, there is a signpost that says: "nächste Strasse links," next street on the left. It says street but it is in fact a farm road, wide enough for a tractor, which leads to the edge of the forest.

In Oberholz, go past a lake whose name I was unable to find. Continue your walk through fields and forests and past the Barchetsee and you will reach a railroad track. Follow the track to the right until you get to a bridge for cars. Here, leave the path that leads straight to Stammheim and take the path that goes across the bridge in the direction of Waltalingen–Guntalingen.

At Schwandegg castle, you have a very nice view of Stammheim, which is on the opposite slope. In the middle of the plateau, you will see the Stammheim hop plantations.

Follow the many bends through Guntalingen. From the center of the village, follow the footpath in the direction of Stammheim Station. This leads directly to a farm that has its own brewery and store. If you feel like making a little detour, you can visit the educational trail through the hop field.

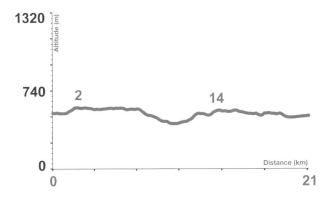

RETURN

The path leads from the farm to Stammheim station, on the Winterthur–Stein am Rhein train line. It will take you about 15 minutes to get there.

HOPFENTROPFEN
Kollbrunn 422
8476 Unterstammheim/ZH
052 745 27 19
www.hopfentropfen.ch

INTERESTING SIGHTS
·   Lake Guri, a marsh of national value
·   Educational trail through the hop field

SUNNENBERG

FROM THE TOSS TO THE KEMPT

ZH

STARTING POINT	**DESTINATION**
# WILA	# ILLNAU
BEER	**DIFFICULTY**
ILLAUER PUNT	
MAP	**HIKE**
# SHEET 226	
(RAPPERSWIL)	**LENGTH OF THE HIKE**
	# 4H30, 16KM
INTERESTING SIGHT	
PANORAMIC VIEWPOINT FROM SUNNENBERG	**DIFFERENCE IN HEIGHT**
	CLIMB 460 M
	DESCENT 520 M

BLONDE
NON-FILTERED
NATURALLY
CLOUDY

5.0% ALCOHOL CONTENT

 PALE GOLD

 TANGY

MALTY

BITTERNESS   SWEETNESS

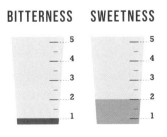

DESCRIPTION OF THE JOURNEY

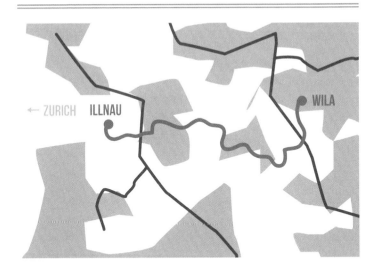

← ZURICH   ILLNAU   WILA

You get to Wila by taking the S-Bahn from Zurich (line Winterthur–Rapperswil).

From the station, follow the hiking path in the direction of Ravensbüel. It goes on the Sunnenberg and offers a magnificent panorama of the Töss Valley and the Alps. Then, continue your walk up and down over the hills for a short distance through the vast landscapes. You will climb a wooded hill as you advance from one village to the next:

→ From Ravensbüel to Hermatswil,
→ From Hermatswil to Gündisau,
→ From Gündisau to Madetswil,
→ From Madetswil to Mesikon.

Shortly after Mesikon, the path veers away from the road and makes it way back to the Brandbach river. Further down, you cross a small bridge which takes you to the first houses of Illnau.
Walk diagonally down the slope until you arrive on the road Illnau–Fehraltorf, which you need to cross.
Continue on the path until you get to an underpass. Here, you can either go right to the restaurant Rössli, or turn left to the restaurant Frieden. Both serve Illauer Punt beer.

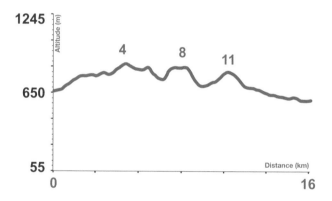

RETURN

From the underpass to the Illnau train station is about ten minutes.

RESTAURANT RÖSSLI
Kempttalstrasse 52
8308 Illnau
052 235 26 62
www.roessli-illnau.ch

RESTAURANT FRIEDEN
Usterstrasse 6
8308 Illnau
052 346 11 58
www.frieden-illnau.ch

ILLAUER PUNT
www.illauer.ch

INTERESTING SIGHTS
- Panoramic view from the Sunnenberg
- The Brandbach River

THE BEAR PIT

FROM THE KRAUCHTHAL SANDSTONE ROCKS TO THE BEARS OF BERN

BE

STARTING POINT	DESTINATION
KRAUCHTHAL	**THE BERN BEAR PIT**
BEER	DIFFICULTY
TRAM-MÄRZEN	**ALPINE HIKE**
MAP **SHEET 243** (BERN)	
SHEET 233 (SOLOTHURN)	LENGTH OF THE ALPINE HIKE **4H30, 16KM**
INTERESTING SIGHT	DIFFERENCE IN HEIGHT
TROGLODYTE HOUSES	CLIMB 530 M DESCENT 600 M

5.1% ALCOHOL CONTENT

BROWN
NON-FILTERED
NATURALLY
CLOUDY

 AMBER

 MALTY AROMA

 FULL-BODIED

BITTERNESS

5
4
3
2
1

SWEETNESS

5
4
3
2
1

DESCRIPTION OF THE JOURNEY

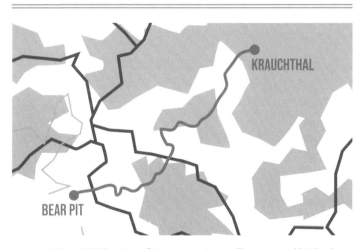

KRAUCHTHAL

BEAR PIT

Krauchthal (585 m) → Chlosteralp → Bantiger (947 m)
→ Deisswil → Ostermundigen → Berne (540 m)

Krauchthal is on the Hindelbank–Bolligen post bus line,
which is part of the Bern S-Bahn (regional train line)
network.
The entire trail is signposted in yellow, but you will
need to be surefooted for the first part of the ridge.
That is why this hike is classified as an alpine hike.
You need to be especially careful when the paths are
wet.

Krauchthal also has its own breweries. The local beer is called Hardeggerperle and can be bought at the Volg store. The store is located near the post office on the road to Bollinger.

From the Krauchthal post office, follow the footpath in the direction of Bantiger. The path quickly leaves the main road and leads off to the right toward the foot of the ridge. After climbing for a few meters, the ridge becomes narrow. The path winds its way between very imposing sandstone formations. Certain sections are made safe with metal cables. A natural cave has been turned into a residence, called Fluehüsli. When you reach Chlosteralp, the ridge widens out and makes it easy to reach Mount Bantiger.

The top of the mountain is wooded. You can enjoy a magnificent view up by climbing onto the viewing platform.

When you begin your descent, choose the path that heads towards Deisswil. It crosses the village of Bantigen at the Brügstock-Beizli, passing by the farm shop, then goes down to the street between Flugbrunnen and Ferenberg. Cross the street and pick up the path again in the fields.

In the middle of the field, there is an unmarked fork: take a left. The rest of the trail to Deisswil is easy to follow.

When you get to Deisswil, climb up a staircase and continue through the woods towards Rüti, then make your way between the houses in the direction of the bus stop until the footpath towards Steinbrüche Ostermundigen turns to the left. It will lead you through the forest and the closer you get to the town, the more paths you will see towards Ostermundigen. At each intersection, follow the signs for Ostermundigen Bus until you reach the edge of the forest. From then on, follow the path in the direction of the Bear Pit. The path goes though some local streets, then up onto a wooded hill and finally past some old villas before reaching the Pit, which overlooks the banks of the Aare River.

The old tram depot next to the park no longer has any trams but has been converted into a brewery where you can drink Tram-Märzen beer.

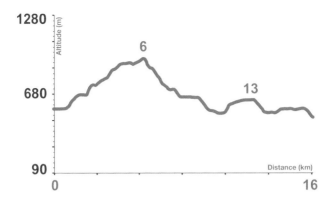

RETURN

Take the number 12 bus towards Bern central station. The bus stop is by the bridge. You can also cross the Aare River by taking the Nydeggbrücke bridge and head through the streets of the old town straight to the station. This will add about half an hour to the hike.

VOLG KRAUCHTHAL
Länggasse 17
3326 Krauchthal/BE
034 411 14 64

BRÜGSTOCK-BEIZLI MIT HOFLADEN
Bantigen
031 931 49 67

ALTES TRAMDEPOT BRAUEREI, RESTAURANT
Grosser Muristalden 6
3006 Bern
031 368 14 15
www.altestramdepot.ch

INTERESTING SIGHTS
- Troglodyte houses
- The viewing platform
- The Bern Bear Pit
  www.baerenpark-bern.ch

THE CRYSTAL
CAVE OF KOBELWALD

**CONCRETIONS, SPARKLING CRYSTALS
AND AN UNDERGROUND RIVER**

SG

STARTING POINT	DESTINATION
OBERRIET OR BRÜLISAU	**BRÜLISAU** OR OBERRIET
BEER	DIFFICULTY
APPENZELLER BIER	**ALPINE HIKE**
MAP	
SHEET 227	LENGTH OF THE ALPINE HIKE
(APPENZELL)	**4H45, 13KM** VISIT OF THE CAVE NOT INCLUDED
INTERESTING SIGHT	DIFFERENCE IN HEIGHT
CRYSTAL CAVE	CLIMB 1000 M DESCENT 500 M

4.8% ALCOHOL CONTENT

BLONDE NON-FILTERED NATURALLY CLOUDY

 GOLDEN-YELLOW

 FRESH

 FULL-BODIED, MALTY

BITTERNESS

5
4
3
2
1

SWEETNESS

5
4
3
2
1

DESCRIPTION OF THE JOURNEY

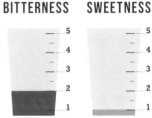

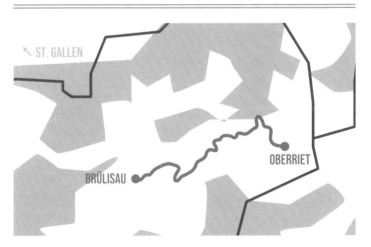

ST. GALLEN

OBERRIET

BRÜLISAU

Oberriet Moos (426 m) → Grotte de cristal (Kristallhöhle) → Chienberg → Strüssler → Montlinger Schwamm → Zapfen (1286 m) → Chli Rossberg → Fulen → Brülisau (925 m)

Oberriet Moos is on the bus line Buchs SG–Altstätten.

The itinerary is well marked but the signs are often partially erased, which makes reading them a little difficult.

From the bus stop, follow the hiking trail in the direction of Kristallhöhle, the crystal cave. It is, of course, marked in yellow, but there is also a big hand-painted wooden sign. One minute later, take the path going in the direction of Freienbach. At the next fork, the Kristallhöhle is once again indicated. The path leads through a small valley and passes a forest before arriving at the entrance to the cave, which can be visited. The trail is well maintained and is more of an adventure than more traditional caves; you'll feel a little like a spelunker. The walls of the cave are covered with sparkling crystals, interspersed with stalactites and a river flowing down below.

After visiting this fairy tale kingdom, climb back up to the surface and take the path in the direction of Chienberg until a trail branches off toward the panoramic viewpoint of Salchet. You must be surefooted for this detour. The view extends over the wide Rhine Valley and all the way to the Austrian Alps. On a clear day, you can even see some of Lake Constance. From this viewpoint, continue climbing directly to the Chienberg, then take the direction of Montlinger Schwamm. There is also a magnificent view from the Chienberg, this time up the Rhine Valley.

During your descent, from the Chienberg, you will come to a sign with no information, which points towards Montlinger Schwamm. Continue on this trail for ten minutes. At the next sign (pt. 783), the direction Montlinger Schwamm appears again. After crossing a scattered forest and some meadows, you arrive at the mountain inn of Montlinger Schwamm. Now, follow the path for Brülisau. In Kriessner Schwamm, you have two options to go to Brülisau. Take the trail that goes straight ahead and you arrive at the Zapfen pass. The view of the Alpstein is fantastic from the pass.

You can continue enjoying this view until you get to the mountain Chli Rossberg. From there, there are two ways to get to Brülisau. Take a right on the natural path. It crosses a ravine and leads to Brülisau, descending along the right bank of the stream. Just before Brülisau, the stream has carved a wild gorge.

You'll find Appenzeller Bier at the Gasthof Rössli, conveniently located near the post bus stop in Brülisau.

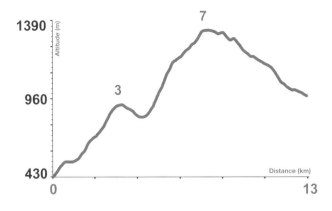

RETURN

From Brülisau, take the post bus or the PubliCar (an on-demand bus service) going to Weissbad, where there are train connections for Appenzell (Appenzellerbahn).

Itinerary 2: Brülisau –Oberriet
You can do this hike in the opposite direction.
The beer from the Rheintaler Sonnenbräu brewery can be found in Oberriet Moos in the restaurant «Schäfli.»

RESTAURANT SCHÄFLI-MOOS
Buchwaldstrasse 21
9463 Oberriet
071 761 11 31
www.schaefli-moos.ch

GASTHAUS RÖSSLI
Dorf 2
9058 Brülisau
071 799 1104
www.roessli-ai.ch

INTERESTING SIGHTS
·   The Crystal Cave
    www.kristallhoehle.ch
·   The farmhouses of
    Appenzell in Brülisau.

THE FLON

VD

STARTING POINT	DESTINATION
GRAND MONT	**LAUSANNE FLON**

BEER	DIFFICULTY
LES BRASSEURS DE LAUSANNE	**HIKE**

MAP	
SHEET 261 (LAUSANNE)	LENGTH OF THE HIKE
SHEET 251 (LA SARRAZ)	**3H15,13KM**

INTERESTING SIGHT	DIFFERENCE IN HEIGHT
THE SIGNAL	CLIMB 220 M DESCENT 440 M

4.8% ALCOHOL CONTENT

BLONDE
NATURALLY
CLOUDY AND
TOP-FERMENTED

 LIGHT BLONDE

 AROMATIC SPICY

 MALTY, CEREAL

BITTERNESS   SWEETNESS

BITTERNESS: 5 4 3 2 1 (filled to 1)

SWEETNESS: 5 4 3 2 1 (filled to 2)

DESCRIPTION OF THE JOURNEY

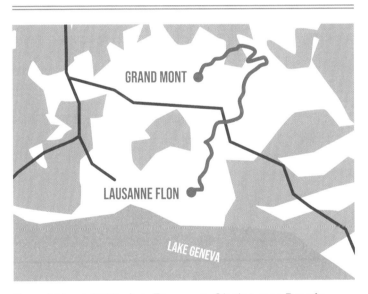

Grand Mont (700 m) → Etavez → Chalet aux Bœufs
→ Fontaine des Meules → Les Buchilles → Le Flon
→ Lake de Sauvabelin → Le Signal → Lausanne Tunnel
→ Lausanne Flon (479 m)

Take the subway M2 to the station Riponne-Maurice
Béjart and then take bus number 8 to Grand-Mont to
the end of the line.

At Grand-Mont, follow the hiking trail in the direction of Chalet des Enfants. This trail follows the road until the bus stop Etavez (about 5 minutes).

You can take bus number 60 for this portion, but it doesn't run very often, especially during the weekend. Shortly before Chalet des Enfants, turn right onto a path in the direction of Lausanne-Tunnel. After about 10 minutes, you will come to an intersection where three roads and three paths meet up. Roadwork is currently being carried out here and there aren't any signs. I took the path to the left (chemin de Liaises) and turned right at the intersection in the direction of Les Buchilles. When the roadworks are finished, you should be able to go straight on in the direction of Les Buchilles. But the little detour is likely prettier.

At the Buchilles, continue on through the forest and then along the forest's edge before making your way downhill to the Flon, which winds through the woods. You have to cross it several times. Next, the path crosses under a highway bridge and you climb a staircase leading to the Forest Reserve of the Old Oaks. The oak trees, which are hundreds of years old, are protected here.

After going by Lake Sauvabelin, you arrive at a panoramic observation tower from where you can see the city, the lake, and the Alps. After a short descent, you reach the Signal, offering a similar view.

After crossing a park, make your way down to Lausanne Tunnel, where the hiking trail ends.

Here, continue in the same direction on the street la rue du Tunnel until la place de la Riponne (white signs for the parking lot). Cross the square diagonally and walk past the post office, then take the street la rue de la Madeleine, go across la place de la Palud, and take the street la rue du Pont, which finally leads to the street rue Centrale. Take a few steps to the right to arrive at the Les Brasseurs restaurant.

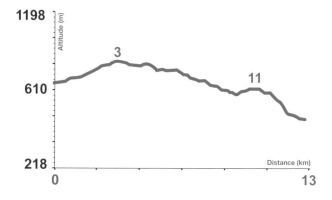

RETURN

From the Les Brasseurs restaurant, continue on the street rue Centrale, go under a bridge, and you will arrive at the subway station Lausanne-Flon (about 150 meters). The line M2 in the direction of Ouchy goes to the Lausanne station.

LES BRASSEURS
Rue Central 4
1003 Lausanne
021 351 12 67
www.les-brasseurs.ch

INTERESTING SIGHTS
*   The Forest Reserve of the Old Oaks
*   The Signal

THE LÄGERN

PANORAMIC VIEWS FROM THE RIDGE OF THE LÄGERN

AG

STARTING POINT	DESTINATION
DIELSDORF	**BADEN**
BEER	DIFFICULTY
LÄGEREBRÄU	**ALPINE HIKE**
MAP	
SHEET 215	LENGTH OF THE HIKE
(BADEN)	**4H, 13KM**
INTERESTING SIGHT	DIFFERENCE IN HEIGHT
THE LANDVOGTEI CASTLE OF BADEN	CLIMB 530 M DESCENT 570 M

5.2% ALCOHOL CONTENT

NON-FILTERED NATURALLY CLOUDY BOTTOM-FERMENTED

 BLONDE, NATURALLY CLOUDY

 SCENT OF MALT

 FULL-BODIED

BITTERNESS   SWEETNESS

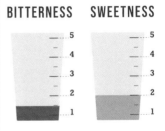

DESCRIPTION OF THE JOURNEY

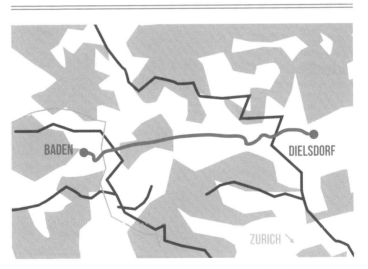

Dielsdorf (429 m) → Lägern (866 m) → Baden (385 m)

From the station in Dielsdorf, follow the hiking trail in the direction of Baden. After a short walk on the sidewalk, the trail bears to the right. You will reach the main road via a pedestrian street and a small neighborhood street. After that, you start climbing. After passing the last houses, cross the vegetable gardens and vineyards in Steinbruch, which is known for its many fossil discoveries. After 40 minutes, you arrive in the small medieval town of Regensberg. If you'd like to avoid the climb, you can take the bus from Dielsdorf to Regensberg. Go through the small town via the road, until the edge of the forest. There, the path bears to the right. Wide forest trails will lead you up the ridge to Hichwacht. You reach it in an hour from Regensberg where you can take a well-deserved break at the restaurant or on the observation deck. Continue the walk, passing by the ruins of Altlägern. The ridge and the trail become narrower and narrower. Fifty minutes after leaving Hochwacht, you arrive on the Burghorn, where it's worth taking a second break. To the south, you can see the Alps, and the Black Forest to the north. After a short descent, you arrive at the narrowest section of the ridge. If you aren't surefooted and have vertigo, bypass the trail a little further down (indicated). When the trail is wet or covered with snow, it's even advised to mountaineers and experienced climbers to take the bypass as the limestone rocks have been polished by thousands of shoes.

After this key passage, descend the ridge at a steady and slow pace until the restaurant Schloss Schartenfels. Walk around the castle and take the stairs down to Baden. When you arrive at the Landvogteischloss (Landvogtei Castle), take the covered wooden bridge to cross the Limmat and cross the old sector of the town to reach the station.

Beer from the Wettingen brewery, the Lägere Bräu, is served in many restaurants. You can find the complete list of restaurants on the brewery's website.

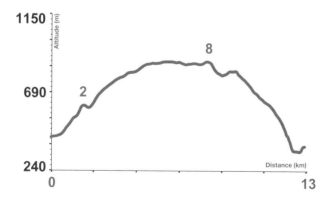

RESTAURANT SCHLOSS SCHARTENFELS

056 426 19 27

www.schloss-schartenfels.ch

LÄGEREBRÄU

Klosterstr. 40

5430 Wettingen

056 426 19 54

www.laegerebraeu.ch

INTERESTING SIGHTS

- Regensberg, a small medieval town
- Landvogtei Castle of Baden

THE LIMMAT VALLEY

THE LIMMAT VALLEY: SHORES, VINEYARDS, FORESTS, AND FARMS AT THE GATES TO THE CITY

ZH

STARTING POINT	DESTINATION
KILLWANGEN SPREITENBACH	**BUCHEGGPLATZ IN ZURICH**
BEER	DIFFICULTY
START	**HIKE**
MAP **SHEET 215** (BADEN)	
SHEET 225 (ZURICH)	LENGTH OF THE HIKE **4H15, 18KM**
INTERESTING SIGHT	DIFFERENCE IN HEIGHT
A BURIAL MOUND FROM THE IRON AGE	CLIMB 390 M DESCENT 310 M

5.0% ALCOHOL CONTENT

HEFEWEIZEN, UNFILTERED WHEAT BEER

 GOLDEN

 BANANA

 FRUITY

BITTERNESS

SWEETNESS

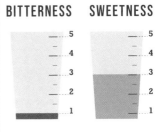

DESCRIPTION OF THE JOURNEY

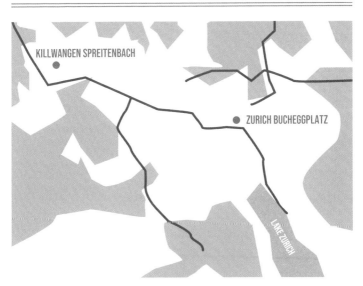

KILLWANGEN SPREITENBACH

ZURICH BUCHEGGPLATZ

LAKE ZURICH

Killwangen Spreitenbach (393 m) → Weiningen
→ Grünwald → Chäferberg (562 m)
→ Zurich Bucheggplatz

Killwangen-Spreintenbach is on the railroad line going from Zurich to Baden.

At the train station, take the hiking trail along the banks of the Limmat in the direction of Dietikon until you have gone under the highway. From there, follow the path in the direction of Kloster Fahr. It passes the bridge and then turns right onto a narrow path between the reeds and trees when going up the Limmat.

After about half an hour, a path branches off to the left in the direction of Würenlos, Wettingen and Baden. This path takes you across a street and then along the edge of the forest until arriving at the next marker, which is about 10 minutes away. Here, take the trail in the direction of Oetwil, Geroldswil and Weiningen. An arrow on a tree points to a pole on the edge of the road and there is a sign on this pole. The pole is in front of a small group of bushes. Here, there is no side road. Continue on the street Waldstrasse until the lake. At the lake, turn to the left in the direction of Altberg, still on the street Waldstrasse. After about 500 meters, at the following intersection, go in the direction of Weiningen. A short distance later, continue going in the direction of Weiningen.

Between Äschbrig and the Hasleren, there is an unrestricted view of the Alps and you will find yourself in front of a sign indicating two options to go to Weiningen.

Go straight ahead, going between Hasleren and the Altberg. You pass the Zangenmoos marsh and go down to Weiningen.

In the village, follow the signs in the direction of Bus until you reach the street Regensdorferstrasse. Turn left here, in the direction of Zurich Höngg. After the church, leave the main road. First take a narrow street and then climb the steps. At the top of the steps a marker indicates Engstringen to the right and only Wanderweg (walking path) straight ahead. Continue straight ahead and when you get to the vineyard, take the side road to the right in the direction of Zurich Höngg. After going through the vineyards and passing the farms, you will reach the bottom of Gubrist. There is a very pretty view of Zurich and the Alps until you enter the forest. Cross the forest and you will come to the restaurant Grünwald. At the Grünwald bus stop, cross the road and continue in the direction of Zurich Bucheggplatz, which takes you to a burial mound from the Iron Age. A short distance later, leave the forest and follow the impressive ridge above Höngg. At Kappenbühl, the town improvements association of Höngg built a rock garden. For more information about these stones, you can make a detour and get a brochure at the Ortsmuseum Höngg (local museum).

Cross a road via a bridge and then another road via the underground passage. You arrive at a farm which has an automatic milk dispenser. If you insert coins, you can have some nice fresh milk. You need to have your own container.

At the next junction, take the path towards Waid, which passes an allotment garden before curving right and down. After a short staircase you turn left. You'll see Bucheggplatz on the signpost. After about 100 meters you'll find yourself on the Waidbadstrasse/Obere Waidstrasse junction. Above and to the left, hidden behind vines, you'll find the restaurant Die Waid, where you can enjoy Turbinenbräu.

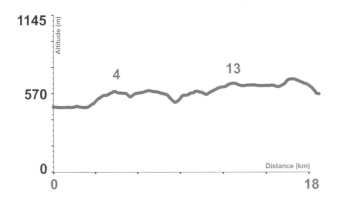

RETURN

From the terrace, take the steps down and then head left of Obere Waidstrasse to Bucheggplatz. After a good kilometer branch off to the overpass leading to the tram stop. At the tram stop there's a signpost to Oerlikon, which you only see at the last moment. From Bucheggplatz there are many tram and bus lines in all directions.

TURBINENBRÄU
Badenerstr. 571
CH-8048 Zurich
043 422 0808
www.turbinenbraeu.ch

DIE WAID
Waidbadstrasse 45
CH-8037 Zurich
043 422 0808
www.diewaid.ch

INTERESTING SIGHT
*   The biotope marsh Zangenmoos
*   The burial mound from the Iron Age and the rock garden

THE SIGNAL OF BELMONT

A WALK IN THE LEISURE ZONE NEAR LAUSANNE

VD

STARTING POINT	DESTINATION
BELMONT- SUR-LAUSANNE	**CLAIE-AUX-MOINES**
BEER	DIFFICULTY
PÉPITE	**WALK**
MAP **SHEET 261** **(LAUSANNE)**	LENGTH OF THE WALK **1H, 4KM**
INTERESTING SIGHT **THE VIEW**	DIFFERENCE IN HEIGHT CLIMB 210 M DESCENT 25 M

5.5% ALCOHOL CONTENT

TOP-FERMENTED

BLONDE

FRUITY, CITRUS

REFRESHING

PÉPITE

BITTERNESS

SWEETNESS

DESCRIPTION OF THE JOURNEY

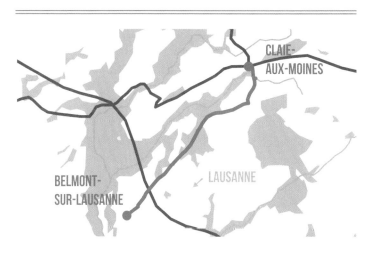

CLAIE-AUX-MOINES

BELMONT-SUR-LAUSANNE

LAUSANNE

Belmont-sur-Lausanne (619m) → Signal de Belmont → Claie-aux-Moines (806m)

Belmont-sur-Lausanne Center is on the bus line Pully–Grandvaux. At the station of Lausanne, take the M2 subway to Ours and then take bus number 7 for Val-Vert, where you get off to take bus number 47 in the direction of Belmont.

At the bus stop Belmont, follow the walking path in the direction of Claie-aux-Moines.

Down to the left, you can see the city of Lausanne and the Jura. After the Signal of Belmont, go through the small woods to arrive at a plateau from where there is a splendid view.

Just before Claie-aux-Moines, you will see a long red-brick building with big windows on your right. The front of the building is black and it has the numbers 39-57.

The brewery Docteur Gab's has moved to Puidoux, but you can find their beer by continuing on the path for about 200 meters to the main road. Here, you will see the bakery Duvoisin on a street-corner to your left. This bakery sells Docteur Gab's beer (all varieties are not always available).

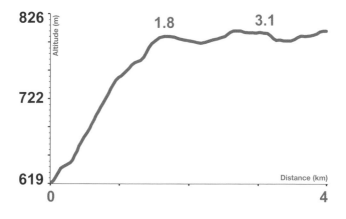

RETURN

Right next to the bakery is the bus stop Savigny, Claie-aux-Moines which is on the line Mézières– Lausanne Sallaz. At La Sallaz, take the subway to the station of Lausanne.

BREWERY DOCTEUR GAB'S
Route de la ZI du Verney 1
1070 Puidoux
021 781 30 90
www.docteurgabs.ch

BAKERY DUVOISIN
Rte de la Claie-aux-Moines 20
1073 Savigny
021 784 25 58
www.boulangerie-duvoisin.ch/savigny.html

THE SOUTHERN
LÖTSCHBERG RAMP

VS

STARTING POINT	DESTINATION
HOHTENN	**AUSSERBERG**

BEER

SUONEN PERLE

DIFFICULTY

ALPINE HIKE

MAP

SHEET 274

(VISP)

LENGTH OF THE ALPINE HIKE

4H, 9KM

INTERESTING SIGHT

SUSPENSION BRIDGE OVER THE JOLIBACH

DIFFERENCE IN HEIGHT

CLIMB 350 M
DESCENT 470 M

5.3% ALCOHOL CONTENT

BROWN
NON-FILTERED
NATURALLY
CLOUDY

 AMBER

 FRUITY

 MALTY

BITTERNESS   SWEETNESS

5   5
4   4
3   3
2   2
1   1

DESCRIPTION OF THE JOURNEY

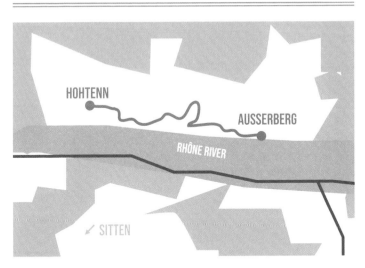

Hohtenn (1078 m) → Lidu → Jolischlucht
→ Bietschtalbrücke → Ausserberg (932 m)

Hohtenn (flag stop) is on the old line from Lötschberg
Bern–Brig.

The southern Lötschberg ramp is part of the Valais
Sun Trail and it well deserves its name. You can find
yourself bathed in sweat even in the spring or late into

the year. For this reason, plants and animals rarely seen in Switzerland can be found here. The trail is accessible from spring until the end of October (depending on the weather). The trail is closed in winter. Information is available at the BLS travel center in Kandersteg, tel: 058 327 41 14.

From the station in Hohtenn, follow the ridge trail of the southern BLS ramp. When you arrive above the hamlet of Lidu, turn right in order to cross the suspension bridge. The trail will lead you downhill. Then, continue on a flat trail alongside an irrigation canal in the mountains. You need to be surefooted. You will come to the gorge of Jolischlucht, which is crossed by taking the suspension bridge.

Once you've passed the bistro ChrüterBeizli Rarnerchumma, you arrive on the tracks of the old industrial railroad going to Bietschtal. You mustn't stop here because of the risk of falling rocks. You don't need a flashlight to go through the tunnel because it isn't very long. You soon reach the elegant Bietschtalbrücke. Cross the high valley above Bietschbach by following alongside the railroad on a fenced-in footbridge.

Soon afterwards, you arrive above the Rhone Valley and see, when looking below the tracks, the new line from Lötschberg which disappears into the mountain. Next, continue on the trail, up and down the hills, until you reach Ausserberg. You can have the beer Suonen at the Bahnhof hotel in Ausserberg.

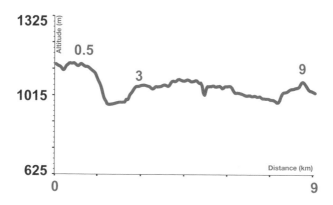

RETURN

Non-stop trains for Brig and Bern from the Ausserberg train station.

CHRÜTERBEIZLI RARNERCHUMMA
076 464 56 90
www.rarnerchumma.ch

HOTEL BAHNHOF
3938 Ausserberg/VS
027 946 22 59
www.hotel-bahnhof.com

SUONEN BRÄU
Raaftstrasse
3938 Ausserberg
079 408 19 68
www.suonen-brauerei.ch

INTERESTING SIGHTS
- The mountain irrigation canal
- The suspension bridge over the Jolibach
- The Bietschtal Bridge

TIERSTEINBERG

ON THE WOODED HEIGHTS OF THE JURA, PASSING BY
THE CASTLE RUINS IN THE FRICKTAL

AG

STARTING POINT	DESTINATION
TECKNAU	**GIPF-OBERFRICK**
BEER	DIFFICULTY
TIERSTEINER BRÄU	
MAP	**HIKE**
SHEET 214	
(LIESTAL)	LENGTH OF THE HIKE
	5H45, 20KM
INTERESTING SIGHT	DIFFERENCE IN HEIGHT
SOLAR CALENDAR	CLIMB 630 M DESCENT 700 M

**BROWN
NON-FILTERED
NATURALLY
CLOUDY**

 BLACK

 SPICY, ACRID

 **SPICY,
AROMATIC**

BITTERNESS   SWEETNESS

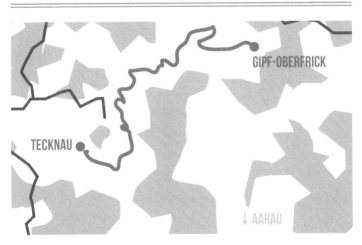

DESCRIPTION OF THE JOURNEY

GIPF-OBERFRICK

TECKNAU

↓ AARAU

Tecknau (445 m) → Ruine Ödenburg → Wenslingen
→ Rothenfluh → Roti Flue → Uf der Flue
→ Tiersteinberg (749 m) → Ruine Tierstein
→ Ruine Homberg → Gipf-Oberfrick (375 m)

Tecknau is on the railroad line Basel–Olten.

From the train station, follow the path to the right
leading out of the village. An old sunken lane begins at
the edge of the forest and climbs until the ruins of
Ödenburg. There, it's worth taking a break to enjoy the

view. From the ruins, continue in the direction of Wenslingen. The marker near the post office indicating Rothenfluh is slightly bent.

In front of the post office building walk up the Mittlere Gasse to the left. The first marker, on the fountain basin, is visible from the post office. The path leaves the village and then turns slightly to the right onto a paved road. Go under the high-voltage lines and continue on until a group of trees at the top of the hill. There, turn left onto the dirt path and follow it until the edge of the forest. Take a narrow trail to go to Rothenfluh. Once you're in the village, turn left to get to the next sign, which indicates Rothenfluh 2 min. Follow this direction to the right. After about 10 meters, turn right again. After 10 more meters, climb to the left in the direction of Rothenfluher Fluh (Roti Flue on the map). The path will lead you uphill and then branch off into a flatter trail to the right and a steeper one to the left. Take a left and climb to the forest's edge. You will come to Roti Flue, a viewpoint with a small bench and a place for a fire. The detour to see the solar calendar (10 minutes round-trip) goes by some very interesting crevices. Continue following the hiking trail in the direction of Wegenstetter Fluh (Uf der Flue on the map). It is a viewpoint overlooking Wegenstetten – with benches, of course. A short distance after Uf der Flue, the path descends until a fork. Take a few steps to the right in the direction of Buschberg. At the next marker, which is nearby, take a left in the direction of Tiersteinberg. After walking on the ridge of Tiersteinberg, which has several viewpoints, you arrive at the castle ruins of Tierstein. There is only one spot where the marker isn't clear, when the blue sign in the direction of the trail to Fricktal shows one direction and the yellow sign another. This is not a problem as the trails meet a bit farther along. You are free to choose. The blue route is a little shorter, but it is steeper. At the ruins of Tierstein, there is also a rest area with fire-pits. In warm weather you can often see lots of lizards.

Next, the path climbs slowly in the direction of Ruine Homberg, the next viewpoint. Walk on the ridge and then make your way down to Gipf-Oberfrick.

You leave the forest at Dürstli. First, the path passes through meadows and a new district, finishing in the old part of Gipf-Oberfrick, where it becomes a wider street. After a few meters, it turns to the left. Leave the hiking trail here and walk straight ahead directly to the bus stop Rösslibrücke. If you're lucky enough to have arrived during the opening hours you can buy the beer direct from the brewery. Turn right by the bus stop and you'll reach the brewery in about 500 meters.

Outside of opening hours you can take the bus to Frick Unterdorf. There is both a direct connection and one where you have to change buses. You can finally enjoy a beer at Bistro Piazza on Frick's main street.

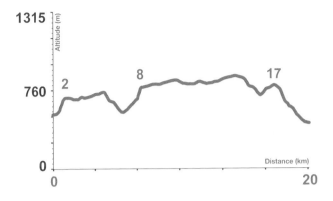

SHORTCUT

Instead of going to Wensligen by foot, you can take a post bus from Tecknau.

RETURN

From the bus stop Rösslibrücke, post buses go to the station in Frick or in Aarau via the Benkerjoch.

CAFE & BISTRO PIAZZA
Hauptstrasse 35
5070 Frick
062 871 62 90
info@piazza-frick.ch
www.piazza-frick.ch

TIERSTEINER BRÄU
Landstrasse 92
5073 Gipf-Oberfrick
062 871 05 70
tiersteiner-braeu.ch

INTERESTING SIGHTS
- The castle ruins of Ödenburg
- The solar calendar
- The castle ruins of Homberg
- Castle ruins of Tierstein

WACHTHUBEL

HIKING AT A HIGH ALTITUDE IN THE EMMENTAL

BE

STARTING POINT	DESTINATION
TRUBSCHACHEN	**WALD BEI SCHANGNAU**
BEER	DIFFICULTY
RÄBLOCH	**HIKE**
MAP	
SHEET 244 (ESCHOLZMATT)	LENGTH OF THE HIKE
	4H45, 14KM
INTERESTING SIGHTS	DIFFERENCE IN HEIGHT
THE EMMENTAL FARMS	CLIMB 800 M DESCENT 570 M

4.5% ALCOHOL CONTENT

NON-FILTERED BOTTOM-FERMENTED

 DARK BLACK

 FRESH

 CARAMEL, COFFEE

BITTERNESS

	5
	4
	3
	2
	1

SWEETNESS

	5
	4
	3
	2
	1

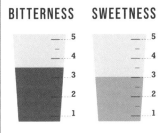

DESCRIPTION OF THE JOURNEY

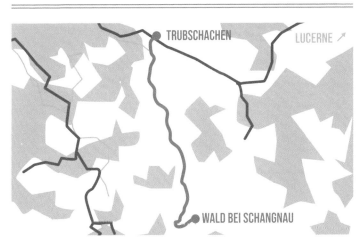

Trubschachen (732 m) → Houenenegg → Vorder Rämisgumme → Pfyffer → Wachthubel (1415 m) → Chüng → Wald (974 m)

Trubschachen is on the railroad line between Bern and Lucerne, going through the Entlebuch.

From the station, take the path until Vorder Rämisgumme. After the Ilfis River bridge, there are three trails to choose from.
I will describe the itinerary using the trail in the

middle via Unter Houenen.

Climb to the Houenenegg, which has a few bends along the way. Then, continue going south along the mountainside. At Vorder Rämisgumme, continue on and cross the Pfyffer. You arrive at the café Grosshorben, which caters to hikers, before arriving at Wachthubel. The view in all directions becomes more and more beautiful as you make your way progressively up the mountain.

At the summit of Wachthubel, you stand facing the Hohgant, the mountain that gave its name to the brewery of this hike. At Wachthubel, take the descent in the direction of Schangnau, which passes via Chüng. This path leads through the forest down the side of the mountain.

Once you arrive at the foot of a small cliff, you will see two forks to the left, one right next to the other. They both lead to a pasture a short distance away. Continue straight ahead, and after about 1070 meters, the trail meets up with the path. Here, there is a marker on a metal pole. Leave the path and take the unmarked trail to the left which leads to the edge of the forest. Then go down through the meadows until you get to the road Schangnau-Wiggen. Turn left and follow the road for about 600 meters until you arrive at the village of Wald. The Hohgant brewery and its tavern are on the right-hand side of the road.

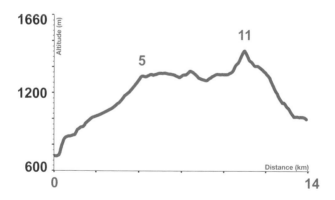

RETURN

From the brewery, it takes about 2 minutes to get to the post bus stop Wald which is on the line Kemmeribodenbad–Escholzmatt. The post bus goes down the valley.

WANDERCAFÉ GROSSHORBEN
034 491 13 02

BRAUEREI HOHGANT
Wald
6197 Schangnau
034 493 30 05
www.brauerei-hohgant.ch

INTERESTING SIGHT
· The Emmental farmhouses

WEINLAND

THE HIKE WITH FIVE PONDS

ZH

STARTING POINT	**DESTINATION**
# REUTLINGEN	# WINTERTHUR
BEER	**DIFFICULTY**
## STADTGUET	## HIKE
MAP	
# SHEET 216	**LENGTH OF THE HIKE**
# (FRAUENFELD)	# 5H, 20KM
INTERESTING SIGHT	**DIFFERENCE IN HEIGHT**
## THE OLD TOWN OF WINTERTHUR	CLIMB 290 M DESCENT 300 M

4.8% ALCOHOL CONTENT

BROWN
NATURALLY
CLOUDY
AND BOTTOM-
FERMENTED

 BLACK

 ROASTING AROMAS

 LIGHT

BITTERNESS SWEETNESS

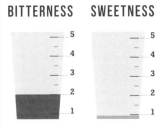

DESCRIPTION OF THE JOURNEY

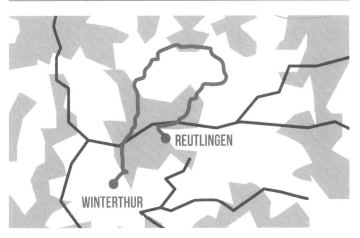

Reutlingen (400 m) → Stadel → Mörsburg → Rietmüli
→ Rickenbach → Eschlikon → Bänk → Seuzach
→ Winterthur/Lindspitz (440 m)

You get to Reutlingen by taking the S-Bahn from
Zurich.

The entire trail is very well indicated and is primarily
made up of unpaved paths. Follow the path in the
direction of Stein am Rhein. It passes via Stadel
before climbing up to Mörsburg, from where there is a

very beautiful panoramic view. Continue on the path and you arrive at the bobsled run of Zurich's bobsled club. At Rietmüli, you will see a pond with an old mill to the right of the road.

Shortly before Rickenbach, you arrive at the second pond with water lilies and reeds. Once you have passed Rickenbach, branch off onto the path going in the direction of Thalheim. This trail leads to a long range of hills with a magnificent view from the top. Next, go down until the railroad line Winterthur–Stein am Rhein. Take the underground passage and continue straight ahead in the direction of Eschlikon, where you will find the Gurisee. The Gurisee is the most beautiful pond of this hike. Its marsh is of national value and a habitat for rare birds. It is located north of Welsikon in Buchholz. Although it is marked on the map 1/50,000, its name doesn't appear on the map.

Follow the path through the nature reserve. This path takes you along the most beautiful shoreline of the lake and then to the edge of the forest, from where you continue in the direction of Seuzach. Go past a bench and you will come to the next pond, simply called Weiher (pond in German).

Next, follow the railroad line until the station of Seuzach. Take the underpass and continue in the direction of Walcheweiher, Winterthur. After going under the noisy highway, you reach the Lindberg and its beautiful mixed forest.

Walk along the rows of hundred-year-old redwoods until you arrive in Walcheweiher. Here, turn right in the direction of Lindspitz. At the bus stop Bachtelstrasse, take bus number 3 to go to the station of Winterthur.

In the old town, near the station, you can have the beer Stadtguet in many different bars and restaurants.

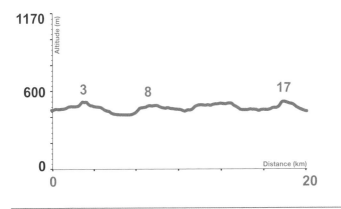

AVEC
Kiosk und Imbiss
Bahnhof Seuzach
052 335 48 60

BRAUEREI STADTGUET
Industriestr. 35
8404 Winterthur
079 784 96 22
www.stadtguet.ch

INTERESTING SIGHTS
- The bobsled run of Zurich's bobsled club
- Gurisee Pond, with its marsh of national value
- The old town of Winterthur

ZÜRICHBERG

HIKING IN THE FOREST AND IN THE CITY
FROM STETTBACH TO OBERSTRASS

ZH

STARTING POINT	DESTINATION
STETTBACH	**ZURICH** OBERSTRASS
BEER	DIFFICULTY
LINDE HUUSBIER	**WALK**
MAP	
SHEET 225 (ZURICH) MAP OF ZURICH	LENGTH OF THE HIKE **1H30, 6KM**
INTERESTING SIGHT	DIFFERENCE IN HEIGHT
IGEL & NATURPFAD, HEDGEHOG AND NATURE TRAIL	CLIMB 220 M DESCENT 170 M

4.7% ALCOHOL CONTENT

BLONDE NON-FILTERED AND BOTTOM-FERMENTED

 ORANGE

 SPICY

 MALTY

BITTERNESS | **SWEETNESS**

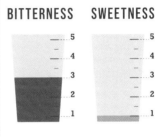

DESCRIPTION OF THE JOURNEY

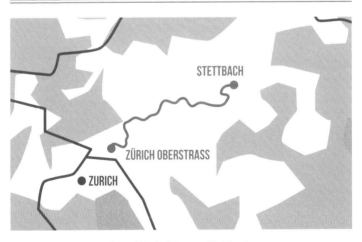

Stettbach (440 m) → Zürichberg (648 m)
→ Moosholzweiher → Rigiblick → Linde Oberstrass

You get to the station of Stettbach by taking the S-Bahn in Zurich, or tram number 7.

Take the trail going by Zürichberg in the direction of Rigiblick.Shortly before the edge of the forest, take a moment to enjoy the magnificent view of Schwamendingen. Next, you follow a wide, comfortable forest trail which passes by Zürichberg and by the

Moosholzweiher until reaching the upper cable car station of Rigiblick, where the marked path ends. The view of the city, the lake and the Alps is particularly beautiful from this spot. Turn left onto the street Freudenbergstrasse and continue on it for about 300 meters until the Spyristeig descends to the right. You will see this street name at the last second.

Continue going down the Spyristeig, and then the street Spyristrasse. On the right-side of the street, there are information signs for "Igel & Naturpfad," the hedgehog and nature trail. After crossing the street Gladbachstrasse, the street Spyristrasse becomes the street Vogelsangstrasse, which you follow to the right until the street Winkelriedstrasse. Take a left and walk down the street Winkelriedstrasse. Cross the street Universitätstrasse and you will arrive at the restaurant-brewery Linde Oberstrass.

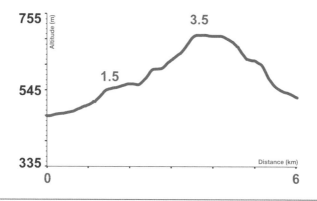

RETURN

The tram stop Winkelriedstrasse is located directly in front of the brewery. To get to the station in Stadelhofen, take tram number 9. Then take tram number 10 to get to the station in Zurich or in Oerlikon, which is in the opposite direction.

RESTAURANT BRAUEREI LINDE OBERSTRASS
Universitätstrasse 91
8006 Zurich
044 362 21 09
www.linde-oberstrass.ch

INTERESTING SIGHTS
- Igel & Naturpfad, the hedgehog and nature trail

5

INDEX

HIKES

BEERS

Adler Panix-Perle	Pragel Pass	182
Albertus	Chasseral	58
Amboss Amber	Entlisberg	74
Appenzeller Bier	The Crystal Cave of Kobelwald	226
Buechibärger Bier	Bucheggberg	54
Bärner Müntschi	Lake Wohlen	154
Bürchner Bier	Hochastler	110
Chopfab	Pfaffhausen	178
Eidgenoss	Babental	42
Entlebucher Original	Haglere	102
Flösserbräu Original	Geissberg	86
Freihof Lager	Salpeterhöhle	206
Fri-Mousse	Gottéron	94
Hopfen Bräu	Stammheim	214
Hübelerbier	Krauchthal	130
Illauer Punt	Sunnenberg	218
Kündig Bräu	Eetelweiher	70
L'Eau de Rose	Ajoie	26
La Fraîcheur	Aiguilles de Baulmes	22
La Marmotte Blanche	Lake Tseuzier	150
La Molardière	Rhone	190
La Rousse Croix Blanche	Sarine	202
La Salamandre	Doubs	66
La Vouivre verte	Areuse	38
Les Brasseurs de Lausanne	The Flon	230
Linde Huusbier	Zurichberg	262
Lonzi	Freiamt	82
Luzerner Bier	Chrüzhubel	62
Lägerebräu Original	The Lägern	234
Maisgold	Roggenstock	194
Monsteiner Huusbier	Fanezfurgga	78
Müller Bräu	Homberg	114
Müller Bräu	Heitersberg	106
Napfgold	Huttwil	126
Paul 01	Loorenchopf	158
Pépite	The Signal of Belmont	242
Quöllfrisch	Alp Sigel	34
Räbloch	Wachthubel	254
Rathaus Bier	Michaelskreuz	170
Rekord	Baldern	46
Rugenbräu Lager Hell	Niesen	174
San Martino	Mendrisiotto	166
Säntisbier	Rotstein Pass	198
Schlossquell	Honaap	118
Stadtguet	Weinland	258
Start	The Limmat Valley	238
Steinfels Bier	Hönggerberg	122
Stiär Biär	Lake Arni	146
Suonen Perle	The Southern Lötschberg Ramp	246
Tiersteiner Bräu	Tiersteinberg	250
Tram-Märzen	The Bear Pit	222
Ueli Bier	Bruderholz	50
Unser Bier	Allschwil	30
Urbräu	Gersauerstock or Vitznauerstock	90
Usterbräu Original	Meilen	162
Wabräu	Gurten	98
Wädi-Brau	Sihlsprung	210
XXA India Pale Ale	Rapperswil	186
Zürich Airport Beer	Airport	18

CANTONS

DIFFICULTIES

MAP

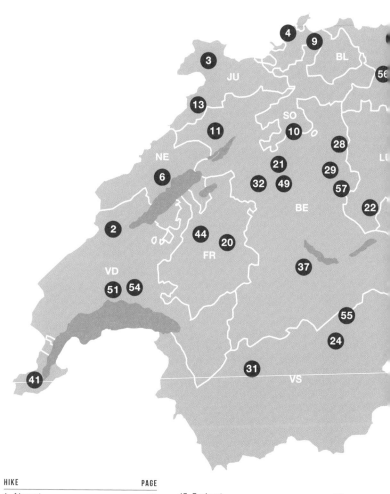

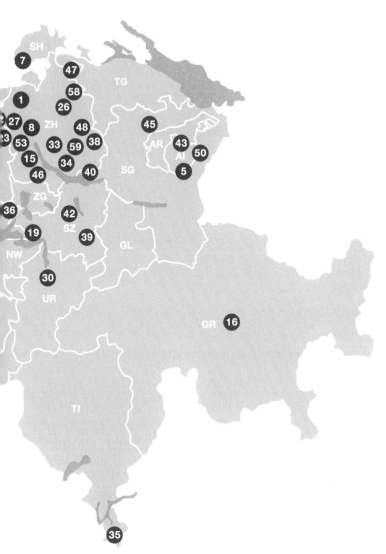

ACKNOWLEDGEMENTS

I thank my parents who taught me about mountain climbing, my life partner Vrene who is with me during most of my hikes and who corrected the inaccuracies and mistakes in my writings, Marianne who also proofread the text, my hiking friends at SAC Baldern with whom I have taken many hikes, the hiking associations for the large network of trails, all the train and bus companies and taxpayers for the public road network, the trade unionists who fought to have more time devoted to leisure activities such as walks, the brewing of beer or the marking of the hiking trails, the women's rights movement which made it possible for women who love beer to no longer be given a dirty look, the topography department for its precise maps, Philipp of the publishing house Helvetiq who published this book, and above all the numerous brewers who have devoted themselves and their free time to the diversity of beer.

Monika Saxer

BY THE SAME PUBLISHER

Swiss Fondue
Jennifer & Arnaud Favre
ISBN 978-2940481-54-5

Grand Tour Switzerland
Hadi Barkat and Sébastien
Pauchon
EAN 7-640139-530707

Fresh Air Kids
Melinda and Robert
Schoutens
ISBN 978-2-940481-62-0

Grand Tour Europe
Hadi Barkat and Sébastien
Pauchon
EAN 7-640139-530561

26 Things to See
Tatiana Tissot
ISBN 978-2-940481-16-3

Beer Hiking Bavaria
Rich Carbonara
ISBN 978-2-940481-82-8

www.helvetiq.com